Past the Horizon

STRUGGLES OF A RESERVED MAN

Raul Leon

Typeset by riverdesignbooks in Adobe Caslon Pro

To my love. To the one I have given so much and wanted to give even more to. I hope our days and memories together can survive past this life and past these pages. I pray that you read this book and can understand me. Even if thousands of eyes gaze at the words on these pages, yours are the only ones I wish have a chance to read this.

– Honeybadger

"You must be ready to burn yourself in your own flame; how could you rise anew if you have not first become ashes?"

– Frederich Nietzche

Contents

Acknowledgement

Thank you to everybody who helped in the making of this book. I tried to make this all a homegrown project looking for people in the local area to help with editing, photography, audio recordings, etc.

To my friends, Ramon, Becky, Ted, Kuljinder, Alana, Adrian, Frank, and countless others who have given me the initial honest feedback, you have all given me the confidence in knowing I can finish this book.

The photography for the front and back cover were taken by a talented local photographer, Cheyenne and I am happy to have found a great photographer with such a distinct style that helped make this book unique in it's own right.

Lastly, to my mom and dad. Thank you for letting me share some of your story and thank you for teaching me so much. I hope I made you proud.

–Raul

Detached

*A*NXIETY COMES AND GOES, *as if like the tides. The moonlight pulls it back and forth. It is mesmerizing as you can see the reflection of the moon glisten on top of the silky ocean. It's dark but still luminescent to the point where you can view the entire coast. A few flickering lights can be seen as if the reflections of the stars come and go intermittently across the ocean surface. Your eyes are encapsulated, fully stimulated, and your feet take a step closer to the water. Your mind believes there is freedom right past the tide, a few yards out. You feel the grains of sand dancing between all of your toes, and they caress your feet in a slight radiance of heat, saying to your skin, "You are home." The breeze blows through and around your skin, and the goosebumps rise to allow for as much contact between you and the air. The feeling of being alone seems to vanish. The wind also brings with it a sweet smell, connecting all your most precious memories with this place as you inhale the soft breeze with each breath. It brings with it a promise, a promise for your soul to rest. That promise seems to become realized as you take more and more breaths.*

Next thing you know, you are halfway submerged in the water. It's not recognized as the water feels as soothing as the wind. As the water pushes and pulls you slightly off balance from the tide, you relax your shoulders. Your muscles all start to relieve themselves, fiber by fiber, from so much built-up tension, and you realize that you feel lighter, almost weightless. You continue to walk, up until the depth of the ocean floor leaves only your head above the surface. You stop to try and embrace this fully. As you do, your mind reduces all of your thoughts but one. You think, "I could die here," *but not out of some sense of panic, rather relief. The gateway to alleviate all of your problems in this physical world is a few feet away, just a little deeper. As that thought lingers in your mind, you pose the question to your entire being,* "Are you ready? Is this it? Are you done?"

Your body, aching and sore, responds first with little hesitation and full conviction, "Yes." *Your mind follows with a similar vigor to that of your body's response,* "Yes." *Your soul is last. There's a bit of silence, as it needs time to process this, as the peace in this environment is so decadent. This silence seems to last hours, as if God himself permitted you this moment to ponder, to present to yourself the true answer. The air seems still, the tide subsides slightly, and the moon even seems to stop, all as a sign of respect to you. Then, finally, when the silence seems a bit too long to bear, your soul speaks and says, definitively,* "No, we are not done."

Time begins to tick again, and your body and mind seem to build a bit of resentment towards your soul. So you turn back to shore and notice your steps are slower, consuming more effort than when entering. Your head is down as your mind and body say their goodbyes to an old friend, one that feels too soon. Your body takes its time to leave as it is disappointed by the answer.

You are finally out of the water, and the breeze dries your skin. You realize how cold your body has become, and this reinforces that disdain you have. "So close, we were so close," *your mind thinks as you endure the evaporation of the soothing water from your skin.*

You finally dry and start to head home. Before you do, you take a final glance at the beach. As you take the last few breaths of fresh air, you realize something. You realize how strong a grip suicide actually had on you. You stop. Immediately, you fall to your knees as you shed tears. You grow disappointed with yourself, and all those initial reactions to your soul have vanished. You quickly release all the disdain and resentment and apologize to it as you finally grasp how it saved you. No apology you say seems to be worthy enough of acceptance. But as you plead to your soul, it responds to you and says, "Its ok. We can mourn for a bit, but get up, we are not done." The tears continue to fall, but you gain the composure to stand. Your first few steps feel like your two feet are nailed to the earth. The weight of guilt, of disappointment, flood you.

*As you are ready to collapse to the floor again, you hear a unique voice, one distinct from your own self. "**Walk. Now is the time to walk. Reduce yourself to a simple being. Let the only thought in your head be walk.**" And those words fill your legs with just enough energy to take a step, and then another. With each step, that weight of suicide, of depression, of anxiety, all lessen, but by only by a feather. However, it is still noticeable, even if it is only slight, as your body is suspended in a state of full awareness. But you don't rejoice. You know how fragile your knees are, and so you must stay focused. That voice comes back again and says, "**Walk. Walk until your legs are strong enough to carry this weight. Walk until your shoulders are strong enough to hold your head high. Walk. Walk to regain yourself.**"*

Time passes, maybe a day or two since the visit to the beach. The intensity of that moment still resides in me; however, the memory comes with a slightly duller sensation. I try not to focus on it, but it continues to linger in the back of my mind as I wonder, *Am I strong enough? If I go back there again, will I be strong enough to pull myself back again?* My mind draws a blank when trying to answer, so I compartmentalize and throw it to the back of my mind, creating a bit of chaos as I do so. So to fight it, instinctually, my body fidgets to forcefully distract me from that memory. I don't know what to feel or think at this point. I am still in shock. My mind seems to be suspended in a position between the past and present. That moment grips me so much that I can't recall of any other memories prior to that.

Each hour passes with that memory anchoring me, almost yearning for me to go back. I look around my room seeing glimpses of that memory, being triggered with almost anything as my mind is actively making connections to remind myself of it. I try to stay occupied in any way possible, but with my body fidgeting so much it makes any task I do much more difficult. My concentration is dulled, and my mental capacity is not up to par. This creates more tension in myself, as my body wants to move, almost uncontrollably, but my mind wants to wander back to that place. I bounce around starting up different chores and tasks throughout the day as my mind cannot stay focused on something for too long. I realize I've taken too many things on at once, and I can't finish them in the time I initially allotted. But I continue on. As the day goes by, I am able to chip away at all those little chores, cleaning, laundry, groceries, cooking, etc. Everything I do today seems hollow. It seems like these tasks don't even need to be done. Their sole purpose is to pass the time, to distract myself.

The sun begins to fall, and the stars present themselves, and the moon relieves the sun for the night. It seems like when the sun was up, it provided my body the yearning to move. But as the moon rises, my mind is what finally receives sustenance. My body loses its grip on my mind as it has expended its energy during the day, and now my mind has free rein to wander to the valleys that hold these thoughts and memories. The moonlight is the catalyst to the honest conversations with myself and evaluate some festering ideas or thoughts. This time, there is only one memory in the queue, the beach. Nothing prior to that moment seems to even matter. I want to ask how I got there, what led me to that place. These questions have merit, but I feel it is not the time to answer them. The real questions I need to answer are, "Where do I go from here? Where am I supposed to go?" Direction. That is what I need. I need to know where to walk and for how long. Destination, "Where am I supposed to go?" This beach, it means something, something more than the place where I almost gave up. So to try and find out, I allow myself to play that memory again. It feels just as vivid as the day I lived it. My mind wants to dive again, but I try and stay composed, so that I can stay separated from that memory. "I am only a spectator, nothing more," I say to myself. And so, as I see this person, this reflection of myself, walking into the water, I feel that darkness hovering over me again. This time its grip is not as strong, but I remember how tantalizing it felt in the moment. I gaze at the ocean surface and notice that flickering light again. I believe it to be the stars dancing in the night sky, but I analyze further. I notice it has a consistent rhythm. On—off—on—off—on—off, and so on. I try to investigate the scenery a bit further to determine the source. And as I do, I notice a silhouette from a distance, right before the horizon. My mind finally puts two and two together and realizes it's a lighthouse. It evaded my focus last time as I was encapsulated by the temptations of death, but my eyes still were able to store its image.

As the cycles of the light continue, I get drawn to them more and more. I ask myself, "Is that where I need to go? Is that where my life lies?" As I ask that question, it syncs up with the pause in the memory. God has granted me the time again to answer this, but from a new vantage point. My soul is the only thing to answer, as my body is resting and my mind is the vessel. And so, I hear from it, "Yes. That is where your destiny lies."

I ponder this for a moment and ask myself repeatedly, "Is this truly my destiny?" as if to cast out any doubt. Every time I ask myself this, my soul responds with a resounding yes. I close the curtains to that distinct memory, as two feelings fill me: excitement and fear. The excitement comes from my soul finally able to picture at least some kind of path to follow, a dream. In the past, it has pushed me to try and answer these questions, but it has received no answer. Finally, after so much time avoiding this question, I was forced to answer. It pushed me to a place where I almost collapsed, breaking myself down to the point of almost nothing. Only after doing so, could I be free to answer it truthfully. And as ashamed as I felt for allowing myself to reach that point, I gained a resurgence of vigor in my soul. It energizes me and makes me want to swim across the ocean right now, but fear is what pulls me back. This fear isn't artificial or self-made, meaning it is not formed from any negative feedback or vicious cycle. No, this fear is primal, as if facing a predator or foe that you know is greater than you in every domain. But what is that foe? The ocean. The strong current coupled with the evolving tides are able to take me at any moment. I've realized this almost instantly, as if a divine moment of intuition. It will be my biggest obstacle to be able to trek along the surface of that ocean, an ocean full of my regrets, sorrows, pains, willing to take me at any moment.

So this is my prerequisite before beginning this pursuit of my destiny. That requirement, "To build my mind and body to withstand the poisons of fear and still move forward." I must build myself from that broken man at the beach to something almost too great for this world to hold. I must build myself to a being that can conquer the ocean. But how do I do that? How do I even embark on such a task? How do I transcend to a being that is fully realized? Nothing comes to mind. It seems like that journey to that lighthouse will need to be postponed. How do I build myself up without knowing what I'm building? Or with what material? But the biggest question of them all, what's in my way? I stand up from my bed, head to the closest mirror, and see the reflection. A question comes to mind. "Who are you?" Silence is all that I hear. I see this character and he is familiar, but only just. We share the same face, the same body, but nothing more. I ask again, "Who are you? "Again, I hear nothing.

I analyze these questions, and the more I do, the more strain I put on my brain. I want the answers to them all. It fuels a fire inside of me. So to help quell it, my mind repeats these questions over and over again, to the point of exhaustion. My body takes over again, again instinctually just like earlier this morning, and fidgets. My mind is asking for new stimuli in order to give myself new information in the hopes of finding the answers I desire. But no matter how much I fidget or move around, nothing is able to bring out an answer. After a few hours, I resign myself for the night.

As I head to my bedside, I feel a small glimmer of hope that my dreams will provide something for me, even if just a clue. And at the moment I lay down my head, I feel a sense of delight. It's small but still present, and big enough that I am able to notice. I ask, "Why do I feel this? And why now?" The answer is simple enough for my mind to reach, even though it is exhausted. Just one night ago I felt the deepest sorrow, the greatest drift and detachment from this world. Just one night ago, I felt death hover over my shoulder, as if consoling with an old friend. But tonight, still feeling all of that despair has sparked just enough light in my soul to cast out my demons, at least for the night. Tomorrow when I wake up, I know they are likely to be back, and just as strong as the night, but I only want to focus on tonight. It feels like with this dim light I can illuminate the first few steps of this journey. The journey will soon start, and it excites me. However, right now, the body must rest so that the mind can temporarily lose its tether to this world and enter the domain of dreams. Soon, I will find the answers. I'm so sure of it that it's almost ironic. Just one night ago, I wanted to give in, to let the ocean take me and never come back to shore. But today, I set my mark past it, to a place I don't know, but with a yearning to find out.

Upon waking, my body is stiff and sore, and my muscles are restraining from moving. I've grown accustomed to this, but my mind feels slightly refreshed. It feels as if just having the spec of hope allowed my mind to actually rest. And upon my waking moments, I try to recall any dream I had. I try to keep those images floating in my head or else they will soon dissipate without the sustenance of mental focus. As I try to recount any images, they all seem scrambled, pixelated in a sense. No image is truly clear and no matter how hard I try to clear that fog, those images stay ambiguous. It deflates me a bit, as I had hoped to be able to find some new clues to answering the questions I posed myself last night. So I decide to get up out of bed with two prevailing thoughts in my head, one of the beach and the other of the lighthouse. Those seem to be the only two sharp images in my head, and they will linger until I have conquered them. These answers will not merely present themselves, I am aware enough to know this, so I get up.

I first make my bed, but with a bit more diligence in making sure it looks presentable, even if only to myself. I look around the floor and tidy up any misplaced shoes or clothes, things that I would normally would leave as they are. Not much is out of position after all the cleaning from the day before. Next, I go to the bathroom and wash my face with soap and scrub with a little deeper scrub, being sure to hit the crevices with more intention. I brush my teeth for a little bit longer and more thoroughly than usual. All of this is done in response to trying to answer those questions, "Who are you? Who do you want to be? How do you realize your potential?" Regardless of what I think that answer may be, or what the process is to find that answer, my standard of being, of living, must elevate as well. My mind is responding to the stimulus of these questions, almost forcing upon me this elevated standard.

I dress myself and decide to actually style my hair, something I have barely done recently. I wear a newer polo shirt. It's black with a good taper from my shoulders to my waist and drapes over my chest well, to create an illusion of a thinner waist as my stomach presides just behind it without touching. The sleeves ride a bit higher than normal showing off a bit more curvature of the arms and the tattoo sleeve that covers my left arm. I wear denim jeans that have a tapered fit to show off a bit of the muscles in my legs. I work out enough to have built a strong physique and decide to present myself in a dignified manner to be able to show off a bit of that progress.

I glance at the mirror and don't recognize who I see, for he seems like a façade. Doubt creeps into my head, asking, "How long will you be able to pretend this person is you?" I don't proceed to answer it. I compartmentalize, something I have grown to be good at. I continue to look in the mirror and overanalyze every flaw of that character in front of me. The question, "Who are you?" pops up in my mind again. I want to go back and get different clothes, some that are a bit more "appropriate for work." Yet the reason I don't is because it would take too much effort. I feel stuck in these clothes and decide to leave dressed as I am. I proceed to put on my work boots. They have some wear on them, and the creases around the toe line are becoming a bit more prevalent. They sit just above the ankle and hug my feet well. They are comfortable at least, but I know they don't necessarily fit with the rest of this outfit.

I open the door and head out of my room, and as I do, a thought pops into my head, *Who am I? I may not know that person in the mirror, but for now, I will act as if we are the same. I will present myself as a confident man, as these clothes require me to do so. When I come home and remove these clothes, then I can come back to being who I am.* It's a proclamation that I will not let the world see how broken I truly am. I'm broken. Finally, I'm not afraid to admit it to myself. My soul has been damaged, but the vigor in myself is in response to the challenge of restoring that broken man so that one day I can wear these clothes again but filled with true confidence. Until then, "fake it till you make it," is what I repeat in my head.

I take some steps downstairs and realize that my stomach is growling. I head to the fridge and do a quick scan of what is inside. Nothing seems enticing for me to eat. I would initially go straight to the cupboard where the Oreos are. I've always had a bit of a sweet tooth, and I would typically want to eat a half dozen cookies coated with a bit of peanut butter. I found this routine to be much easier than my old habit of trying to make a balanced breakfast, so I grew complacent to it. That simple sugar is something my body always can eat and has been something I've had to rely on as of late to have any sense of sustenance. I've tried to make many typical breakfast meals—oats, eggs, toast— but they all seem to not agree with my stomach. But I want to uphold this new standard for myself, so I go and make a bowl of oatmeal and decide to save the cookies for after. Each spoon of oats I ingest makes my stomach more and more uncomfortable, and I wonder why. I grab the box of oats and examine it quickly. I realize that its past the expiration date by over a year. It's really been that long? How bad did I slack on my diet? I stop eating the oats and just pray that it doesn't get me feeling any worse.

I leave for work with my stomach still a bit upset from the breakfast. I pack a few snacks (mainly cookies) to get myself through the day. I feel a bit of dread upon stepping into my truck. I begin the drive to work where I am prepared to spend ten to twelve hours. Each hour I spend there seems to be more and more unfulfilled. The drive only makes me soak up that feeling of dread even more. I see the same dull brown hills and mountains surrounding me in every direction. The Reno skyline can be beautiful, but the drive to work makes it feel like the mountains are closing in on me. I take the longer route to try and find an excuse to not go to work, but I still arrive on time. I wonder why this disdain has been more prevalent than usual and finally make the distinction that it's been the first day back since the beach. In the short time between now and then, I've become further disconnected from everything. As I walk through the front door, nobody really notices anything different neither my demeanor nor my attire. At least, I don't have to put much effort into holding up this façade. It allows me to focus on the job.

I work in an industrial setting, machining cement into specific shapes using very specific material. The entire factory calls them saws, but they're much too intricate to be called something so primitive. Most of the factory contains equipment focused on producing the cement slabs. These machines never seem to stop moving as production needs seem to be more important than human needs. The entire plant runs 24/7 with every hour of the day and every day of the week being covered, even holidays. The scale of that machinery is so much bigger than I have ever worked on. They tower over any person. They reach so high that they almost want to grow past the ceiling. They all work in unison, so it is hard to find where one ends and the other begins. But the machines I am in charge of are not part of this main line. They sit at the end of the factory, as if cast out due to its uniqueness in nature, something I feel we have in common. They take the slabs and cut them to form specific shapes.

The nature of the job is toxic, in many ways more than just physical. The dust created can create very unhealthy conditions in the human body. The machines use specialized cutting blades to make these shapes, one by one as they run down the assembly line. Any noise you make is drowned out from the high pitch of the cutting equipment. I get down to the plant floor where the machinery is and have to be suited up with my hard hat and ear/eye protection. So the hair that I put some effort into making look nice is hidden and will likely be ruined by the end of the day. The plant floor is only a few thin walls away from the outside environment. When the dry heat rises, the plant temperature also does, but with no motion in the air. It is a stale section of the world it seems. The heat cooks you and makes just standing uncomfortable. When the heat leaves during the winter months, your body will react to even the faintest breeze of wind. The temperature drops so low that even the air becomes chaotic, as it fidgets around in an effort to warm itself up. This place is stagnant, as if a physical representation of my state of being. A lot of the similarities have become noticeable, for when that beach almost engulfed me, it shook my entire vantage point. Seeing the same environment with a new lens is a bit eye-opening. I can even notice that the workers all walk as if soul-less beings, robots. No emotions on anybody's face, and with uniforms to make them all look the same. Each person has a distinct silhouette, but they all still look and act if they are the same person.

I look at the shift lead, the man who trained me on the machines I am now in charge of, and I see the same thing. He is a bigger figure, standing a few inches above six feet, and towers over me (I'm only five-foot nine). He has a worn look on his face, as this place has taken a toll on him. The only other distinguishable feature is the size of his arms and hands. It's a product of the countless years of manual labor here. Anything else that is unique about him is lost in the uniform.

He sees me walk in and says, "Good morning, sunshine."

"What's up, Cory? How are you?"

"Oh, you know, living the dream. How was your weekend?" I almost panic as it sparks the vivid imagery of the beach. It is still too fresh in my mind. But I somehow compose myself and respond trying to avoid that topic as much as possible. The environment helps hide some of the instinctual reactions of panic.

"It was all right. Nothing special to note. How did the saws run this weekend?"

"Good. I didn't get a text at all from the crews. What about you?"

I realize that I haven't checked my phone since last week. These machines are new. Since me and Cory are the only ones who are adequately trained on the machinery, we are the ones to be called for help. If we can't figure out the problem, then we typically have to get outside help, and the company doesn't like to exhaust those resources before they exhaust us, literally.

I respond, "I didn't check my phone, but I figured any problem the crews had, I'd walk into them today to deal with. I'll take a look at the saws if I have a chance. Do you know the run schedule?"

"Yeah, you're good to check and do some maintenance. We'll be running the other machines for the next few days. I have to run the shift or else I'd help."

"No worries, man. I'll get to work on it."

Every week, there are a few days that these machines are idle, and it gives me and Cory time to do some maintenance on them, since our maintenance department does not know what to do with this equipment, either. I get to work on doing some inspection and maintenance on the saws. The day is filled with repetitive tasks of checking motors, aligning parts, calibrating the accuracy of the machine, inspecting blades, checking inventories of blades, and a list that would take pages to finish writing. This all has to be done before the next time these machines are set to run, but I can't get it all done today because I have desk work that needs to be done.

The first day of the week, I need to mine data and present it to the managers on how well these machines have been running every week. It takes hours to find the appropriate data, clean it up, and present it to in the format the managers like. With that comes a common theme from the managers that "We could be doing better. These machines need to keep pushing out more product." What they haven't realized is the growth of production has skyrocketed, but how the data is presented it makes it seem like the machines have not changed output. In reality, it's doubled, close to tripled.

The manager's meeting approaches quickly. Time flies after doing all the repetitive tasks. I get the data and set up the presentation in the usual PowerPoint format that they like. I walk in with greasy hands, some holes in my vest and a noticeable amount of dust (from the saws) as I had no time to wash up. I scan the room, and everybody glances at me, some with disdain. I can only assume that they are thinking, "This guy can't even clean up before the most important meeting of the week?"

The meeting details how each department does, and the main line is the center of attention. My part in the meeting is relegated to a mere four or five slides, but as I stated, those four or five slides take hours to present the information that they ask for. As the meeting progresses, my slides are up, and the manager shifts his focus to me. He has a slim figure, but his title holds a lot of power and he isn't afraid to show it. He is also probably the smartest one in the room and will know if any number is off the mark or if there were any corners cut. His concentration in his stare can make even lions tremble, I'm sure.

"All right how did the saws do last week?"

"They did well. There were some issues with a few products not providing us proper cut quality. I think it can be attributed to board quality coming from us by the main line."

He immediately challenges that. "And how do you know it was from the main line?"

I grow anxious as this overpowering figure is in front of me challenging what I'm saying and I begin to stumble.

"Well…uh…It's a bit evident in some of the boards that they…they aren't straight."

"How do you know it's not from the machine skewing the boards?"

"Well…I…I guess I could check some of the drive mechanics."

"Please do, and report back to us next week."

"Copy that."

I know full well that the machine is fine. I just spent half a day in there verifying as much as I could, but his overwhelming presence makes me lose my confidence and back down. I leave that meeting deflated even more, and a whisper of the thought, "Not good enough" plays in my head. I ignore it for now. There's still time left in the day to get some work done.

The work seems meaningless, making high-end product for people who don't know or really care how rigorous the work can be. Everybody here works in the shadows of society, just like many industry jobs. The place adds validation to the nihilistic idea, "You are meaningless, and nothing matters here." That idea has grown a foothold in my mind and reigns dominion over me especially while under the factory's roof. But as I am, something or someone keeps you here. I start to relinquish those ideas for now, as there is work to be done.

Hours pass, and it is finally time to leave. Ten to twelve hours at the plant drains me. I begin the trek back home but seem to always carry a bit of the stress with me. As I drive, I notice that my eyes feel heavy behind the wheel and time is slowed. What usually is a thirty-minute drive back home feels like three hours, almost like work itself is intentionally pulling the clock back just to squeeze a few more minutes of production. After those draining minutes, I finally make it home, and all I want to think about is the next task at hand, showering. I slowly take off my boots and feel like I've lost fifty pounds alone, not just from the boots but also from the sweat I lost during my shift. I realize that I looked too far ahead. Before I can shower, I need to make it upstairs. What would normally feel like an easy task seems like hiking a mountain as my legs have little energy left to carry my weight. I notice that slight bit of hope I had this morning and last night has been drowned out by the all the stresses at work. I don't have enthusiasm to finish the day, so I resort to only willpower and pride. That pride is a vain attempt at self-esteem. It merely tells me, "Get up. This is not the place to quit. Don't show anybody that you're a quitter. You were raised better." So those words fueled me, reminiscent of how my soul carried me away from the beach, and I make it upstairs. I see my bed and am tempted to just fall asleep but remember the standard I started to implement in the morning. Begrudgingly, I stay standing, undress, and turn on the shower. The water hits my shoulders first and alleviates some tension, not all of it, though. But it is enough to enjoy these few moments of free time I have for myself. I get out with my mind and body slightly reinvigorated and still have yet to realize how hungry my body is. It has been patient all day and reduced its yells for sustenance as it too knew that work needed to be done and any distractions would be a hindrance to that.

I get dressed for bed and head downstairs as my body excretes more ghrelin to signal its hunger. I repeat my breakfast, almost exactly. Some oats, a few eggs, and about a half dozen Oreos. It's not fully satisfying, but it's enough to get me through the night. As I finish my last few bites, I start to mentally prepare for another heavy day, but I forget that tomorrow morning prior to work I need to go the gym. The early morning is the only time that I am willing to get up and go. So I set my alarm for a few hours earlier, and instantly a bit of resentment is formed. To think I have to wake up at 3AM to just have an hour to stay physically healthy. It's irked me ever since I started this job a few years ago. But no matter, I see it as work that needs to be done. I walk back to bed, and to my delight that glimmer of hope has returned to me. I remember the excitement I had to want to enter my dreams again, to unearth just one clue to answer these questions in my mind.

Suddenly, I feel the urge to skip the gym to have more sleep but not for any physical sustenance. No this is merely to allow my mind further opportunity to explore that realm of dreams. I want those answers to those questions that are anchoring a part of me to the beach. But I also remember what I recognized this morning of that raised standard. Unfortunately, I deny my soul's request to sleep, for that work needs to be done in the morning. I want my mind to find the answers I yearn for but do not allow it any new resources. I do not have much capacity to reach any further. I have spread my resources too thin already. Something does not resonate as I think. *Have I not tried hard enough? Am I doing this wrong? What am I supposed to do?* The time winds down, so I go to sleep, but now those few thoughts have some company. I stay determined to answer all of them, but for now, work.

It is still the dead of night when my alarm goes off at 3 AM. My body wakes up resentfully, trying to fight me so it can stay in bed and rest. But I force myself up, brush my teeth, get dressed, take some caffeine, and head out the door. Those small processes seem blurry as my mind struggles to keep up with my body. My mind feels like it is moving through a thick heavy fog. It has no recollection of any previous step and needs to concentrate fully to make sure to know where to place the next step. My mind and body have a lag between them. I get in the truck and drive to the gym and get drowned by many old thoughts, memories, and regrets. It's the only time I can feel a bit vulnerable, so I allow myself to indulge in it. I take a glance at my silhouette in the rear-view mirror, and I get the urge to ask myself, "Who are you?"

I hear a response from my heart. "I am you…I am the one who took you to the beach."

I grow infuriated, as if talking to an enemy as I reply, "Are you serious? Why would you even consider that? Why did you drag me there to die?"

"Look at us. Look at everything you're doing to us. You get so caught up in your ego that you're killing yourself anyways, and for what? Nothing. Nothing but pride. And you leave me here in an empty body with nothing to comfort me, with nobody by your side. I had to try and put us out of our misery."

"I don't believe you. I don't trust a single word you say. Get out of my head. I don't need you. I don't need anybody. I can do this alone."

"Keep thinking that and see where it leads us."

That voice dissipates as I near the gym. I think, "This is all fuel." A second thought comes as I get to the gym. *Maybe today I can kill those demons, those old lingering thoughts. If I go just a bit harder, dig a bit deeper, and maybe I can shut out that voice, too.* I hope that maybe by releasing all of my energy with these thoughts as fuel that any remnant of those thoughts will vanish.

I walk through the gym doors, as if entering into a battlefield. The gym is small with new and well-maintained equipment and is a relaxed environment. There's ample lighting everywhere, but I want to battle in the darkness, so I put my hoodie on to drown some of that light from my eyes. The air conditioning is on and the room is in good condition. It seems like a normal, inviting fitness center. But for me, it marks the terrain for internal war. Such a dichotomy, how such an open environment can still be seen as a warzone to some. As I gain fuel form these old regrets, I start to move around. I want to sweat, to leave a pool of it and in it those dead memories. I want that feeling of exhaustion when I leave.

My body now is the one to lag as it needs a small jolt to feel that proprioception. It needs to recognize that it is in a place of movement, that it needs to move here. The warm up begins, and I lie down on a bench to begin training. As more weight gets added to the bar incrementally, my mind dives deeper into those valleys of old memories. *It needs fuel*, I think. I work up to a weight that's resistant, and that's exactly what my body needs to feel awake. I start lifting this weight. As the number of repetitions increases one by one, my mind is presented with a dilemma. The first option, to complete the set and re-rack. The second option, to continue on until I physically can't move this weight. I have this dilemma with each repetition, and with each repetition, I choose the second option again and again. I repeat this cycle until the muscles in my arms cannot fully complete one more repetition, and even then, there is a bit of contemplation as if to say, "Why not, what else is there to live for or preserve myself for?" But I decide to finish the exercise there, for I want to continue that feeling of exertion. The battle has not yet achieved the goal of extinguishing those old memories. Exercise after exercise this dilemma is repeated in an effort to quell that urge to kill those thoughts. Finally, my body reaches the point of mechanical failure. My muscles cannot move anymore weight, even lifting my arms presents a struggle, but that urge is still present. There is still fuel in the reservoir which says to me that those memories are still very much alive.

I can't move anymore weight, so I jump on the treadmill to run. There is not much time to do so as the hour for work soon approaches. So I crank the speed up to a pace that is hard to maintain for fifteen minutes. For fifteen minutes, I run as hard as I can with only one thought in my mind, *Kill. Kill that old self. Kill those old memories. Silence that voice in your heart.* Just by repeating those words in my head, the primal instinct begins to kick in and allows the body to move a bit faster. I run now as a predator chasing prey. As I feel like I have come close to that prey, those fifteen minutes have elapsed, and I grow disdainful. Emotionally, I still ride that endorphin high as I breathe heavy trying to recover air. There is more in the tank, at least that's what it feels like in the moment. Once my body heat starts to drop and

I recover my heart rate from the battle, it's noticeable how tired I really am. I can't move my arms, and my legs feel like gelatin. I feel proud, for I pushed more than most normally would. There is still work ahead of me for the day. I have another grueling shift in a place that is segregated from the world. I reflect on some of the eye-opening things that I was finally able to see and just the thought of going back there deflates me.

I go home and get ready for work. I enter the front door, and the house is still, with even the air being passive. I take my running shoes off and start peeling off the layers of clothes, all coated with sweat. I get upstairs, with heavy legs, and get ready, and a recurring thought pops in my head. "Why…why am I doing this? Why do I make it hard for myself? Maybe that voice was right."

I get in the shower and it refreshes me a bit, as if cleaning off the blood from war. I seem to peel off a layer of myself and renew myself a bit, just so that when I get to work people won't notice that demeanor of the broken man. As I'm getting ready, I reflect a bit on the day so far and recognize that I am intentionally giving myself a crutch, almost as if I need to prove to God that these challenges are too easy for me. I exhaust myself on purpose to make the grueling day even harder. *Throw yourself in the fire*, I think, *but why? What purpose does doing this hold?* My mind draws another blank. I think, *At one point, I would've never asked myself this question. I would have merely put my head down and worked, regardless of how I felt.* That's enough contemplation for now. I have to make it to work on time.

The hours pass slowly, as another lengthy day at work finishes. Much of yesterday's sentiment is still present, and I feel the boring patterns take a toll. I get home and simply want to pass out, but I can't. I remember that today there is martial arts class. Instant dread fills my heart as I don't want to go, but the feeling of creating discipline makes me.

I change my clothes and wash my face slightly and drive over to the dojo. I drink some more caffeine in an effort to be able to keep my eyes awake for the drive. Again, that question I ask is, "Why?" It seems as though I continue to run away from these questions. I know this and want to change this, but I feel as if now is not the time. I don't want that answer to be blank, so I decide to not answer, thinking I found a loophole to the question. *I just want to focus on getting to class*, I think.

Throughout the drive, I try to squeeze out any ounce of motivation to be able to make it through the class. I make it on time, a bit early in fact, and sit in the truck. There is a quietness, a stillness between now and the time class starts. I play some music to fill that emptiness, but a bit of uneasiness grows in my stomach. Shortly after, doubt comes in and says to me, "Just go home. You're tired. You aren't in the mood. Just leave." And I consider it more than I would have liked, but I know that it's partially true. My body is starting to feel drained from the day, but more importantly, my mind is tired. I don't know if I can exert any more energy.

Sheer will is the only thing moving my body now. As the starting time for class approaches, I step out of the car and head into class. I must use each step before I enter the dojo to compose myself, to put up that front of being "ok." I do a good enough job to not pique anybody's attention as I enter. I try to go through class with the same enthusiasm as when I first started this martial art, judo, years ago. I still remember why I joined in the first place, to cover a scar with more pain. But I found some enjoyment in it and decided to continue as a devoted monk does his prayers. I notice that it has been easier to put up this front of presenting myself as ok. I warm up with the team and look around the dojo to gaze at the environment I once called a second home. The feeling of drifting apart made me also drift from this place for a short period of time. But even so, I feel like I've gone too far that no place feels like home anymore, not even the house I bought myself and reside in.

I look around the dojo to see who will be in class today. Looks like there are a few good comrades and the normal lineup of instructors. The dojo is an open space, not many things out of place or in the way. The martial arts mats sit below a high ceiling where if you look up you can see all the rafters. It's a bright room, and it seems like that every crevice is illuminated. The walls are white but full of pictures of past sensei/masters and added ornaments of specific accomplishments of previous and current students. It provides a sense of glory to this place. The mats are a royal blue, only adding to that honor this place holds. They are gentle enough to take impact from, but also distinctly firm. As you slide your feet along them, you feel a faint embossed texture, resembling the stitching that was done to form each mat tile.

Running around doing the warm ups pulls me into a head-space, parallel to the one in the gym earlier. It's a fine line between being mentally present, in the moment, and drifting away into a realm of detachment, to a place of internal warfare. That place flickers on and off in my head. What tethers me to the current moment is the comradery, even if only physical. There are people willing and able to partake in this physical exertion with me, and it mitigates the feeling of loneliness, even if only slightly. Then I remember why I continue doing this sport, for the people. I look at everybody around me, some are older, some are younger, others taller, others smaller. There is such a diverse range of people in this room all willing to do this together, all people I likely wouldn't have met if it weren't for doing this sport. It keeps my head above water and my mind at ease until the class is over. Throughout class, I do all the drills and conditioning diligently, with no cut corners. I gasp for air after so many drills but keep persevering. My shoulders ache and my hands become weak, making it difficult to even grip on my own gi. There's a distinct feeling here. Something I can't quite describe in the midst of "battle." I don't spend much time pondering because I need to just get through class. Persevere, that word continually pops up and is repeated in my mind over and over in an effort to draw energy from it. Finally, class reaches its end, and that first breath after the instructor yells "Sore made." (Japanese phrase for meaning "finished") is so relieving.

As I change and get ready to leave, I ponder "battle." I thought about that word sporadically throughout class. At surface level, I think it only as my mind describing what I just went through, controlled violence. But that explanation still seems hollow, incomplete. I want to wander into my own headspace to keep thinking about this, but the main instructor comes up to me and starts a conversation.

"Hey, good practice today, senpai (a higher-ranking class member). I saw some good hustle and good counter-techniques today. Keep up with the strong gripping techniques and stay active in the sparring rounds"

"Thanks, sensei. I've just been working on trying to keep up with all the other guys. They're all working really hard."

"They see you work hard, too. Don't sell yourself short. Are you ready for the upcoming tournament this weekend?"

I've been in my own headspace so much that I didn't even realize that there was a tournament coming up. I don't want to feel rude or disappoint him so I come up with an excuse on the spot.

"No, sensei, I have to work. I have to cover for somebody this weekend. I'm sorry."

I notice a bit of disappointment in his face as he replies, "Oh, it's all right, senpai. We'll sign you up for the next one. I think that one will be in Las Vegas."

"Ok, sensei. Let me know the dates, so I can let work know which days I need to take off."

I don't want to let him or the team down, but I feel like I am. Being a senpai means to always be a good example for the lower ranks. Lying to my coach makes me feel like I don't deserve the title of senpai anymore. I just want to go home.

As I enter my truck and take a seat, the fatigue has risen to the point where I have to acknowledge it. Adrenaline from the class is the only thing holding the fatigue at bay. I pray that it is enough to get back home safely. As I passively ponder that word "battle," my mind actively runs simulations of what I learned in class. I think of different ways techniques could have been applied or how to make techniques more efficient, as if finding different ways to solve the puzzle. It keeps my eyes awake and attentive for the drive.

The truck is finally parked, and I head back inside. My body has cooled down enough to realize how tired it truly is. There is no more mental or physical capacity for anything else in the day, just as I felt the day before, only the depths of today's fatigue seem to dive a bit deeper. The repetitions of the days are taking their toll. Again, I try to force some food down as I recognize I haven't eaten much all day, and just the energy required to do so becomes more difficult with every bite. I push through and finally am able to head upstairs to close out the day. In the shower, I take extra time, not because the water feels good, even though it does, but because I don't want to move much anymore.

Once I muster up the energy to finish, I head to bed with no thought at all. I have worn myself out completely. The sting of setting my alarm is the last thing I remember feeling that day. It doesn't matter what time that alarm clock is set for. I just want to fall asleep and will wake up when told to do so. Five hours is all that I am given, but those five hours are peaceful and rejuvenating. However, it is not enough to be able to recoup enough recovery from the last few days. I must dig deeper into that pit of fatigue for these next few days.

Four o clock, that's when I have to get up. I fight my body's urges to stay in bed, and even my soul's plea to rest. My pride, my discipline, those are the only things that carry me up and push my body to move. I move with no real intention, with the only objective to keep moving in order to stay awake. Once a few minutes pass, my mind is finally engaged and aware. It notices the drained state my body is in. But I distract myself from this feeling by thinking about what I have to accomplish for the day at work. The sting of just thinking of work is present, just knowing that I have to go back to that miserable place. But even that is more manageable than the overwhelming fatigue of the body. As I drive to work, my mind easily wanders and reflects on the past few days. I recall the memory of the beach. It seems so distant, as if the last few days have wedged so much space between then and now. But it still holds so much value to me. It breeds a fire in my soul, one that makes me want to turn around, leave everything behind, and run. Run towards that dream that burned so brightly days ago. How do I preserve the light of these embers that house this dream? I can't continue to run away from this much longer. But I am chained to work, to the life that I have accepted by inaction. I feel disappointment brewing in my heart, so to combat this, I push this memory back into Pandora's box. I know exactly what I'm doing. I am compartmentalizing again and accepting the consequences. But I know that soon this dream will require more than what I can offer it now.

The effort of driving causes my eyes to feel heavy at times, as it does most mornings, but I still somehow make it to work. Another dulling day as the fatigue in my body intensifies. My mind grows irritable for every small detail. Today is even more gruesome as the saws are scheduled to run this morning. Cory and I have to check everything on these machines and get it all dialed in as soon as possible. And a special guest is at the plant, the vice president of R&D. In the company, he is a step above the plant manager in authority and seniority, only a few spots removed from the CEO. I've never met him nor the CEO, but from what the plant knows, they are scoping out this machine to try and order more for the plant…just what I need more machines to try and take care of.

There isn't much time to set up the machines to run. Even after the last few days of checking the equipment, it's still an extensive process to get it set up properly. All the old blades need to be taken out and replaced with new ones. Since each tool is slightly different, each one has to be moved to the proper position one at a time. This typically can't be done sooner as the production schedule changes on the daily, and we won't know the exact product we need to make until the day of. It takes a lot of skill and a bit of luck to be able to set up these saws quickly. I got good at them by doing it alone for months on end. I had to, or else this place would have gotten rid of me a long time ago. Then, the rest of the production line needs to be set up to handle the product a bit more diligently. It's a high-quality product that is easy to mishandle and is prone to breaking from the rugged machinery, so a lot of tinkering is required to make sure the product gets off the line ok. We have maybe a few hours to get this whole line set up before the R&D director walks through.

I compartmentalize every little feeling or thought so that I can focus on getting this job done quickly, or else I know I will hear it from all the managers the coming week. And suddenly, the heat from the still air loses its potency and doesn't bother me anymore. The sweat from my body goes unnoticed. The aches in my muscles subside, or rather they are ignored. The need to drink or eat is even curtailed. The headache that I've carried since Monday even seems to have temporarily relieved its pressure. I have reached a state of emptiness, of presence, with only just enough focus for the next task at hand that I receive. There are no thoughts of the past or future. It feels like a perverted form of enlightenment, one only stumbled upon by accident. I can acknowledge that there is a beauty to this state of mind, but also acknowledge that this is not true enlightenment. I am not voluntarily present and actively clearing my mind of pestering thoughts. In fact, I do the exact opposite. I am present by obligation to the life I have received, and subconsciously moving all of my thoughts away to allow this feeble state of being the ability to focus its capacity on one thing; one task is all I can manage. In the heat of the moment, I don't question how this came to be. I just graciously accept it as it is what I required to continue to press forward.

Cory and I move with a ferocious pace to get this line set up. I focus on the saws specifically as Cory works on changing over the rest of the line. Sweat is dripping from my hard hat, and he's running around the rest of the line fixing all the minor issues. It took us hours to get that line set up, as it usually does, and as the first few good boards make it down the line, the vice president walks in. Cory and I look at each other and breathe a little sigh of relief before the director approaches us. He is a short and very slim figure. He wears square-framed glasses, and a nice collared shirt with a simple plaid design. His pants look like they're made from silk, and his boots look like he just bought them yesterday. He holds his head high and has a jittery walk to him, as if ready to see what he needs to and get out of the dirty production environment. I whisper a remark to Cory as the director is slowly closing distance.

"Cory, this guy doesn't look like he belongs here, does he?"

"Nope, not at all. That's how all the higher-ups are. I've only met a few but I can tell that this guy's important. Be careful with what you say."

"Copy that."

"Good morning, gentlemen. How are you today?"

I respond first, "We're doing good, sir. How are you?"

I go to extend my hand to greet him. He looks down and refuses, keeping his hands behind his back and moving on to the next thing on his agenda.

"How are these machines running today?"

Cory sees me a bit demoralized so he is able to step in and say, "They're all set up and waiting for you to see them have a go."

"Let's see how they do today."

He asks us both a barrage of technical questions about the saws. His accent makes it hard for us to understand what he is saying, and every time he repeats himself, he gets visibly more frustrated, as his wrinkles on his forehead flare up and his hands start to jitter. Cory keeps an eye on the line to make sure no problems are arising with the crews as I have to try and entertain our guest. It feels like we are treading on thin ice with every question he asks and my mind is starting to shut down. Luckily, we make it out unscathed as he is pressed for time for a meeting.

"All right gentlemen thank you for showing me around, and good luck on the rest of your shift. I'll be in contact with you guys should I have any more questions."

"Thank you, sir. We look forward to having you back soon."

"That was intense right, Cory?"

"Yeah, I can see it in your eyes. He beat you up without even throwing a punch."

"Yeah."

As the workload decreases, I find myself feeling everything that was blocked out earlier, but this time much sharper. The headache slowly creeps back, but with more intention and a greater pressure. My eyes seem to be teary, not because of some emotion, but rather because of the lack of water. The sweat around my body somehow makes me feel heavier, feeling as though that the lack of fluid throughout the day is locking up my joints. The bottoms of my feet feel like I have just finished a marathon. Before I head home, I enter the bathroom to try and clean myself off, for the dust on my face and hands is starting to irritate my skin. I look in the mirror and barely recognize this man. It looks like a version of me that has aged twenty years. There are bags under my eyes. The lack of food and hydration makes my face more sunken and has a quality of malnourishment (probably because I am). My arms look feeble as well, as if the work drained my body of sustenance from any spot it could find. The only good thing I can think of is, *At least I earned my dinner.* As if it was a reward for making it through the day and not a human need to eat. The remainder of my thoughts are filled with just being home and sleeping. I have exerted all of my will to do anything else.

Who are you? That similar voice in my heart emerges. I don't care to hear it now. It seems like that voice is loudest when I'm at my weakest. And each day that passes, its voice becomes louder.

So I wash my face and try to rinse off this overwhelming sense of self-pity. I hope that by cleaning off the sweat that it will take this feeling with it. And for a moment, the instant that cold water hits my face, it does. The refreshing sensation pulls me back to the present moment. I grasp for any little pocket of joy now, as they are rare nowadays. Even the ideas of joy, contentment, and happiness feel so unnatural, so foreign. I have lived a life away from those feelings, almost intentionally, and I have forgotten how they feel. So when the chance is presented to rejoice in them, I still feel a bit of uneasiness, feeling like an unwanted guest, trying not to overstay my already shallow welcome.

The drive brings with it a sensation of melancholy. It has a soothing feeling for me, I notice. It reduces the pain of my headaches and helps me cope with my body's aches. There is no malice in this feeling, only a deep connection to the void in my soul, to the depression in my veins. I initially wonder why I feel this now, but I have suppressed enough for so long that it is merely the steam exiting the teapot when its water has reached boiling. I have grown more sensitive to the inconsistencies of the days. I have grown more impatient with everybody I interact with on a daily basis, which admittedly is a small faction. I notice myself drifting away from those closest to me. It makes me wonder about my family. I haven't talked to most of them in months. I think about my mom and my dad and my two siblings, an older sister and a younger brother. All three of us left Mom and Dad around the same time. It seems like ever since then, all of us have lived in separate worlds. *I have time to call them, Mom and Dad. I should at least try.*

Dad is usually at work so I figured I'd call my mom first. He actually enjoys his job. He's a machinist and makes expensive parts for the aerospace industry. He's always been one to enjoy his work and seems so invested in it. Mom would always tell my siblings and me growing up, "Your dad wouldn't even know I was dead 'til he got back from work. He'd make sure that the funeral is on his lunch break." We all chuckled at it, and Dad would respond, "That's right." He is a stoic man and is always so calm no matter what situation. He's always held my admiration, and so has my mother.

My mom works in quality control for another manufacturing company around the area. Industry jobs seem to run in the family. She is such a detail-oriented person that it suits her personality well. Mom isn't one to enjoy her work too much. She can tolerate it, but that's about it. What she loves are her projects: home improvement, fundraisers, church events, and business ideas. She wants to eventually create her own business, a restaurant. I would back it. She's an amazing cook. She's always been a person to enjoy a challenge and is excited to learn something new, even if she fails at a certain endeavor, she can always smile at the end of the day. They're both great parents, and I almost feel ashamed to be their son. I feel like there is much more to prove in their eyes.

The phone rings as I wait to hear my mom answer. Each ring of the phone makes me a bit more nervous, as if I'm ready to meet my childhood hero. A few more moments pass, and I hear the voicemail prompt. I felt a bit disappointed. I don't know what I wanted to talk to her about, but I was just hoping to hear her voice. I haven't talked to her in a while. I miss her. I miss Mom.

"Hey, Mom. Just wanted to call to see how you're doing. I'm sorry I haven't called in a while, but I'm doing all right. I know I probably missed a few of your calls, so I figured I'd try to call you back. Anyways, don't worry about calling back. I'll try to call you again tomorrow. All right.Love you. Bye."

I hang up and head inside. The uneasiness in my soul allows me to move, not with excitement but with anxiety. When I get inside, I do all of my chores. I try to race against the clock in order to try and get the most rest possible tonight. Finally, when I finish, I am able to lie down and relieve myself of the body pains and the headaches, as the bed caresses me. My body has lost all tension as it slowly settles into a resting position. Before I try to close my eyes for the night, I stare at what's in front of me, the ceiling.

A blank wall, with a knockdown texture common in every house. There is a plain white coat of paint that has a matte finish, which further reinforces the blandness of the environment I am surrounded in. My eyes jump around between various spots of textures on the ceiling, as if trying to examine each one. My mind finds itself at ease from doing this, and I tell myself, "This. This is the highlight of my week." I broke myself down enough to have this as my prevailing thought. The ceiling, so bland, with such uniformity, just like me. A piece of somebody else's puzzle. How did I fall so much? How did I lose such a vibrant spirit? That spirit that was filled with such originality, such uniqueness, such variety. Maybe this is just facing the reality that none of these things were ever really present, that they were just a lie I told myself. Maybe all of this work, all of this physical exertion, has opened my eyes to what the facts are. I need to know that what I've told myself as I have grown up is true. I need to know that who I have been presenting to this world is equivalent to the person I truly am.

With little thought, I know this is not the case. It's like I can see myself being ripped apart in a thousand directions, like every part of my being has a different objective. I've been very passive in my life, in my own growth. I did not trailblaze any path. Rather I have taken the easy one, one that has allowed me to feel safe. I chose a job out of the convenience of not looking for another. I bought my house brand new for lack of willingness to fix up another. Now that I'm aware of this, I keep wanting to dig out these old skeletons in the closet. Each one seems heavier than the last, and it physically hurts. A headache forms again, and I decide to stop for the night. My soul wants to continue, to reveal how deep this divide is between who I am and who the world thinks I am. But I must postpone this for just a few more days, so I can get to the weekend. I promise myself that I will do this, but I need to rest. My body wins the battle as my eyes shut and my arms wrap my blanket around me.

I wake up to another day of blandness. I evaluate the quality of sleep I had last night to see if my body has rested and if it feels recovered. Both seem false. My joints are sore and muscles are stiff, just as usual. It's a surprise to feel refreshed from any rest. It seems that the debt of fatigue is too grand to repay, at least with sleep being the only form of currency to try and repay with. I check my phone to see if my mom called me back. She didn't. I know I told her I didn't want her to call, but I did. I don't know why I said otherwise. I fell back into not dressing myself nice for work, not to style my hair, or act like I'm trying to present myself better. It was short-lived, for I realize that at work nobody ever notices or cares. I spend so much time there that at first it merited the effort to present myself better. But with the actual work I do, it seems pointless to put that effort for those who don't even care to notice. The type of work would also ruin the effort. The sweat and hard hat would push out any product in my hair, and the dirt and grease would only ruin the nice clothes. So I go back to the bare minimum, an old crew T-shirt and some worn denim jeans. They are tasteless and make me feel like another dull silhouette, just like my fellow coworkers. I feel resentment, for I want to present myself in the best way I can, and still want to, but there it is not worth it.

That yearning for me to feel like myself again—or better yet, for the first time—has grown in me. That white ceiling, the one I see every night and every morning, I will no longer be a part of it. That little bit of hope I initially had is starting to show again with a bit more luminosity. Even though my physical state is subpar, my mental capacity is low, and my spirit is worn, I feed on this hope to fill those gaps. And so, the day begins anew. More monotony as I grow awareness of my dull day-to-day life. Monotony and pain, they have been my sole companions for so long. Forever I dare to say. I reflect on these words as I continue on with the day. I notice how far I have drifted into this detached state, one that has kept my subconscious on what once was, that I forgot what being in the moment feels like. "Soon," I keep repeating, "Soon." Soon I will be able to give these questions the time, the diligence, and the focus they deserve. For now, I have to let this desire boil, to concentrate it all, and let it smolder until I can finally let it breathe and grow into the wildfire it was meant to be.

The day continues, and the daily tasks are completed, fixing machines and moving around material up and down stairs. I was taught—or rather told—to do these things: to fix the equipment, to operate it, and to treat them as my own children, although they are never truly mine. They are owned by those above me. However, I do all of these tasks with that diligence of a father, and pride commands me to be disciplined and to do a "good job." I move away from the desire of answering those questions as I start to feel as if these thoughts are visible to those around me. I can almost see the faces of the managers looking in my thoughts and being disgusted for thinking of something other than work. It feels like even my mind cannot be a place of refuge in this environment. I don't want those thoughts and that hope to be tainted, so I force it back as best I can to protect it. This time, it is not a form of compartmentalization, as I acknowledge its place in my mind, but solely a form of protection to keep it pure. That dream has started to grow precious to me, more than I have realized at the moment. With every turn of the wrench, with every speck of dust on my clothes, with every ounce of grease on my hand and every drop of sweat on the floor, that dream, that desire in my soul burns brighter.

Another day finishes, and I realize I am one day away from the weekend. As I am driving home from work, my mom calls me. I feel too tired to engage in any conversation, even with my mother. It's sad to say and even more sad to deny what I've wanted to hear, my mom's voice. I hate this. I wish to just go home, not my house, but home, that small house we all grew up in that's only an hour from the city. The drive is filled with memories I cherish. I open the truck window and can smell my old room. I recall moments with my brother as we shared a room. We both hated our sister a bit since she got her own room. It seemed liked we fought every day over something petty, but we made up at the end of the day. Why can't life be that simple again? Why can't I just go see Mom? I'm ashamed. I don't want her to see her son like this, broken. I'd rather deal with this pity alone. So I just head home and try to continue the rest of the day like this thought never happened. I let the phone ring, knowing I'll miss her, but she leaves a voicemail and I listen to it once I get home.

"Hey, mijo (my son in Spanish). I got your message yesterday. I hope you're doing ok and not overworking yourself. You sounded a bit tired in the message. Anyways we miss you, and we'll be up in Reno this weekend. Maybe you can invite us over for some food, or we can go out and get some dinner. Your dad and I miss you and we love you. Take care, mijo. Call me back when you can. I know you're busy."

I want to cry after I hear that. I don't know why I didn't. Maybe it is pride, maybe it is the dehydration taking away my tears. My heart yells out to me, "You see now? Do you see why I took you to the beach? What are you doing all of this for? Why are you doing this to me?"

I respond, "I'm sorry. I don't know what else to do."

"Do what you want then. I'll just be in the background, rotting. Just forget about me."

Shame is a word that does not merit what I feel at the moment. Depression doesn't even seem suitable. I just want to quit everything right now, but I'm locked in a standstill between my ego and my heart. I wish to find peace for once, but I don't want to let go of anything to do so.

I grow more and more tired of debating myself, and I remember that I skipped working out yesterday and feel the need to do something today. Although I initially dread exercise, I find some joy in it. I use it as a testing ground, one to test my resolve, my discipline. And in moments like this, it helps me quell those various voices in my head. I have set a standard for myself, and I intend to live up to it. So I think about what I should do when I get home, *Weights, running, judo...* Then out of the blue a thought pops up saying, "rest." Upon initial reaction, I am displeased by that thought and respond, "Why rest? You've made it this far. Your fatigue is past the point of recovery. Why not dive deeper? Are you going to disappoint your parents by giving up here, too?" But then I realize what it means. My soul wants me to replicate the desire for my dream. It wants me to hold that urge to move, to allow it to smolder. Let that urge soak in my body just a bit longer and prove to myself that patience will draw my full potential from me. I ponder this realization for a bit, and the more I do, the more I become drawn to that option. And so as I arrive home, and as much as my body urges me to move, I deny its requests. I go about the rest of the day with a calmness knowing I don't need to expend any more energy. I even try to preserve as much energy as I can to be ready for the next morning.

That's when I'll let that dog out. Become unchained, savage, untethered tomorrow morning. The alarm is set for 3AM again, and I get to bed as soon as I can, for the stage of the battle has been set. I lie my head on the bed, look up at that ceiling again, but don't pay any attention to it this time, for I want all of my resources expended tomorrow. As I am lying down, I find it difficult to sleep. I have grown impatient and excited, for I wish to be at the battleground already. The fatigue is overshadowed by that feeling of excitement, but I try to fight it to calm myself and go to sleep. To try and find a way to calm myself, I repeat the word "smolder" as my mind settles more and more after every iteration. My eyes close, and my body rests.

The alarm rings at 3AM, and my eyes open instantly. I hop out of bed as my muscles have been waiting diligently like loyal soldiers to be put to work. I get my daily morning rituals done as soon as possible. This feels like the only thing that has grown excitement in me all week for I have built the anticipation for this. I have tempered the excitement, and now it is time to reap those rewards. I get dressed, I wear my typical grey sweatpants, a bit baggy because I have this thought of not wanting to show-off (even though there are few people awake let alone at the gym at this time). I put on a navy blue long-sleeve crew shirt. It has some miles on it. The color seems faded, and the cotton has lost some of its soft touch and grown to be a bit rough. The armpit stitching is starting to unravel and a hole has begun to form. Still, I wear it, partly out of nostalgia, but also to protect those tattoos on my left arm. I spent much time, money, and pain to gain these permanent forms of art, so as an act of respect to them I wear this shirt. I cover them to care for them and also to not present them to those unaware or unworthy of the meaning behind each one of them. Finally, I get my shoes on, a pair of Converse (Chuck Taylor). They are a newer pair with a lot of traction left on the rubber sole. The shoe itself does not have any excess in materials, with just enough thickness on the flat sole to protect the bottom of the foot from the ground. But I can feel every time that shoe flexes, acting as an extension to my own foot. They are perfect for the task ahead. I want to feel connected to the ground. I want to feel the balance shift across the plane of my feet as I hold the weight in my hands from lifting up from the ground.

The deadlift, such a simple movement, but filled with ferocity. Why? All that needs to be done is pick up weights off the floor and put them back down. That's the extent of this movement. That bar has been there for me more than any person. No other being has the authority to say that. It's a worthy adversary worth every ounce of effort, and it has shown me a glimpse of the true depths of discipline, motivation, and tenacity. It takes the grunt of the punishment that I deal it, and with no quarrels. It invites it even, asking for any worthy challenger. I've built up the motor pattern of that movement to feel natural now-and have done so after years of this repeated motion. There is no wasted thought in how I approach the bar, how I set my feet, or how I grip it. I have transcended all of that, after years of diligent practice, and can now place that mental focus on pursuing the depths of that tenacity, that resolve. Next thing I know, the bar is right in front of me. I don't question how I got here. I merely embrace it. To test this resolve, to feel like my muscles have been appropriately stimulated, I need enough weight on the bar. So I add a pair of forty-five-pound plates, one on each side. With each repetition, I pull the bar to my shins. The bar's knurling digs into my hands deeper. I lift it off the floor as the bar rubs on the bones of my shins, and I fully extend my legs and torso, until I stand upright, and then I drop it controlling it all the way down. Each repetition of this gets me more and more focused. More weights get put on the bar, again in increments of ninety pounds. (Forty-five pounds per side). The heavier weights start to excite my body.

My muscles feel selfish as they want more effort. Three hundred pounds, not enough. Three hundred and fifty, not enough. Four hundred pounds more. Four hundred and fifty pounds good, something worth all the exertion of my body. I know this too as my mind grows anxious. Before I set myself up ready to lift, I sit down. I collect my thoughts as they help confine my anxiety. I tell myself, "Hold no reserves. Set all of your inhibitions free. Let your limits be considered as suggestions. Let that dog out, and unchain him from the tether of these prohibitions."

Suddenly, all of my anxiety has vanished and been replaced with a silent fury. I get set, almost impatiently, but I hold on to this fury until I am fully set, and then finally I lift. That first rep makes my muscles work. The second rep shines light of that insatiable hunger. The third rep pushes my resolve for this weight fights back and wants to pull me down more and more. The fourth rep brings out that dog. The fifth rep and sixth reps seem like blurs. I don't remember how they felt. The only thing I feel now is that wildfire born of that fury, of that ferocity. It's the manifestation of all the haste and hatred I have ever had for myself, all honed for a single objective, to lift, to work, to bleed. I only let go to allow myself to go again. Such energy, such vitality I feel. Upon that moment, I say, "Whatever else this day has ahead of me doesn't matter. I made myself feel alive, and nothing will take that from me." I've given everything I had to this, and whatever recoil, whatever the consequence I am dealt, I deem is worth it for those few moments of living. For the rest of the training session, this feeling of life fills me. I wish to feel this at all times, but I know of the recoil. I have expended all of my resources, all of my mental focus, all of my physical strength, and I know once that adrenaline drops all that will be left will be anxiety and depression. That price for this feeling of vitality is the overwhelming sensation of numbness, to make sure the scales are even, but I don't care. As the training session draws to a close, I have this feeling hovering over me of wanting to fuel this desire to answer the questions, *Who are you? Who do you need to be to get to that lighthouse?* But I can't. I'm stuck with only questions and no answers and no time to ponder them. I wish I had the time to sit down and just think about this, but I have to get to work.

Evaluations

A LMOST A MONTH HAS PASSED since that day on the beach. Those daily, weekly repetitions took their toll on me. The singular moments of happiness and joy were not enough to combat the overwhelming pity and angst. The one thing that has changed between then and now is awareness. The same routine was driving that wedge further into my soul and became so great that it became impossible to not notice. I grew the desire to want to analyze my entire being, from the ground up. No thought or memory is too small to analyze. And so now I am obligated to build the environment in which I am able to do so. I know now that my current state of being is not capable of providing this for myself. So what must change and why? I find myself analyzing this question at every break in this hectic life I live. During the rare breaks at work, during the drives to and from home, during the lulled time right before I go to bed, all are times for reflection. The constant internal turmoil eats away at my pride to the point that it reduces any barriers for internal dialogue. It took many years to build up that shell of pride, the one that hardened my heart and as a result made me fragile. The smaller internal traumas forged the cracks, and the constant pressures of the day-to-day have caused the cracks to creep, to grow, until there was too much damage to try and repair them.

I have grown my awareness this far with the little time I have allotted for this purpose, but they are low-hanging fruit, something that I should've caught much earlier. The true depths of this awareness must be fleshed out with proper time and proper sacrifice. I realize that I must let go of something, or multiple things, even everything if deemed necessary. Nothing is safe to stay if it means it will pull me back into the water. From now on, stay afloat. Right now, I must see what pieces of my life I am free to remove or restructure. So now I lay down everything I do or am tied to and evaluate each one for its purpose in my life. I feel the need to create a bar, a standard on which to measure these things. "What do they mean to me? How much of myself do they require? What do I get out of them? And most importantly, how does this get me closer to that lighthouse?" This mental exercise has taken up much of my focus. My pride has already shattered, and so I feel less inclined to provide for work anything more than it requires. Work has done nothing for me throughout this entire process besides hinder its progress, so it seems like the best place to begin evaluating its meaning, upon a slow time during work.

How did I get to working at a spot in which I am devalued, demoralized to the point of being nothing more than a human body? My specific title is engineer, but that does not seem to fit the job description. It's better to call myself a lackey, one who must deal with the corporate expectations of higher production output, and who has to manage the day-to-day stresses of production. I fell into this field as I never wanted to answer the question, "What do I want to do with my life?" I punted it to my parents and took their insight as law.

I remember helping my dad fix some things around the house. Whenever he would get frustrated, he would tell me, "Son, when you're an engineer, you'll come up with a better idea than this piece of shit."

"Ok, Dad. I'll do my best."

I had an idea of studying criminal justice. I'm not really sure why, but I've always liked the idea of creating fairness for everybody, to help make a just world. I wasn't a popular kid, and I felt like my voice was never really worth listening to, so maybe having authority as a judge, I'd at least be heard. When I told my parents, it didn't seem to impress them at all.

My dad would say, "Really, son? Why would you want to do that?"

I would always choke up when I tried to answer. "Well...I guess I like it. I don't know."

"Listen, son, we'll support you, but is this really what you want to do?"

"I don't know."

So by default, I decided to stick with engineering. It was the one thing that would make them proud and the only thing I believed to be in the cards for me.

I had no idea how far the consequences reached in my life. I did not pay attention to the fact that this may be a focal point of my life for many years. I only thought about what would look like a nice accomplishment and what would make my parents proud. I admired the challenge, nothing more. It was a naïve sense of thinking, but one that has been integral in how I've gotten here in life. I've realized this when dealing with that challenge, when

I was in the trenches of that battle. I knew that I might not have liked this career at the end of my school journey, but what kept me persevering was that old pride telling me not to quit. And so I did, and in that process fell in love with testing myself, not even for pride's sake, but solely for my own.

Upon leaving college, I wondered if this career was really for me. I took a job right out of college that taught me many new skills. There was great joy in that, and I found pleasure in being able to create unique solutions to certain problems. I was able to fulfill my mental stimulus by being able to learn, and my soul felt happy by being able to create things. This was enough to continue this pursuit for a few more years, as I believed that many jobs were similar to this in nature.

My previous job was good. It allowed for many freedoms, but I felt as time passed that my worth was starting to grow past what that place would offer, so I felt the need to leave. It was a quick assessment in what I believed to be my financial value. I wanted more money and did not feel comfortable in asking for it. So I started looking for new jobs that I felt would offer that. Not much was on my mind besides that. I did not fully think about my decision making, I just felt like I wanted a change but did not have the patience to do my due diligence in finding a truly better option. The first job that offered me more money was the place that I decided to go to.

And as a result of this extra income, I decided to take on a bit more financial burden. I bought a house and a truck to prove to myself that I am an adult and that I could handle the extra stresses. Again, this was a challenge to me, to put these crutches on myself, to put this extra weight on my back and still manage the day to day. I didn't care where I was going, only that I did not stay at the same spot. I wanted to feel like I was making progress, but in reality, all I was doing was sinking farther into the quicksand. There was no direction. I didn't even consider it. So the consequences are what I have to deal with now. Work has always been important to me, again as a test of my consistency that I could perform to my capabilities regardless of circumstance. I forced myself to believe that I could do this in my current or former state, but I couldn't. The weight of guilt, of shame, of inadequacy, all soaked and penetrated deeper into my mind as I kept blocking it out, and work was my distraction. This job has been no different, and it fed on that. I allowed it to take more of me than I wanted. And now, I want it back. I want every ounce of effort I gave to this place back so that I can use it on something valiant enough of my efforts.

This job is temporary, for it provides for me only the financial stability, but I have resolved myself to leave, and never come back. For I feel it in my bones, and it aches my heart every time I step foot in that place, the mismatch of ideals, and they have begun to corrupt me into thinking those values are worth staying. But it pushes me farther away from that lighthouse. It begs the question how much my ideals have shifted, how little strength they really have in order for me to drift away from them this much. Conviction is something I have lacked. Something I require to navigate the rough waters if I am to make the journey to that place. I need to find what I truly can stand for and build on in this world. *Who are you? How do you realize your potential?* The answer is starting to unfold. I must put these questions aside for a moment. For although I have committed to leaving, I will commit to this place until I have the ability to be free. I wish to be free from any obligations to pursue what my soul initially found joy in, to create.

One thing I can take away from this job in particular is that I have built even more discipline in working at a soulless, tasteless place, doing work that serves no purpose for me. And so, the day starts again, after this lull in the day, in which I have spent it at my desk. I spend so much time on the plant, fixing the daily issues that I forgot what it felt like to sit in a normal chair in an air-conditioned room. Besides the few times I need to pull data for those weekly meetings, I am always out at the saws, fixing them, running them, or training others on how to run them. My desk is small and has enough room for a computer and monitor and a few books. All the dust from the processing of the cement coats my desk in a layer of it that always seems to build up no matter how many times I clean or wipe it down. Although the room is air conditioned, there is not much else that bodes well for it. It has old carpet that is matted down and stained in various spots, and some stitching is starting to wear causing some edges of the carpet squares to ride up. The color is dark grey, but that seems like the aftermath of years of stains and dirt covering its surface. I can't tell what the original colors are supposed to be. The walls are colored an off-white, but the tint of the light makes them appear as beige. There are multiple spots where the drywall has started to erode, and by the top edges, where they meet the ceiling, water stains can be seen. The gloss finish on the paint dulls the knockdown texture and makes it somehow lose the one piece of originality these walls have. They are thin enough to hear any conversation outside, and it is not uncommon for conversations to pop up that involve some of the engineers in the office. Nobody would know this as no other employee spends enough time in this room to catch this small detail.

I'm sure there have been many conversations about me, but I have not been around to catch them. For that, I am grateful for spending much time out of this room, one where the only window is located on the door. The room is located right across the hall from the employee bathroom. The main pipes from the bathroom run underneath the floor. When proper servicing or maintenance is not done, it fills the room with a rancid smell that I hope I don't have to describe in detail. I share this office with five other engineers, all with similar size desks. We are granted the freedom to arrange our desks as we wish, but we all lost the will to do anything original to our designated areas besides a few people that have been here longer than anybody else in the plant. Each one of our desks seems to pile up with production paperwork and random parts that were ordered.

This is where I spend my downtime. The only reason I feel an ounce of comfort here, sitting in this worn chair with the upholstery starting to rip, is because it is the only place where employees aren't as keen to bother me. Even they don't like to spend much time in this room, no matter how air conditioned or well heated it is. Even at home, I can get bothered from the company emails, texts, and calls, but at the office, I'm allowed just a few moments to recollect myself before heading back to the plant floor.

I walk out of the office now that the lull is over with my head down. One of the newer engineers walks up to me as our paths cross for a moment and says, "What's up with your head down? You won't see where you're going."

I admire his positive attitude. He hasn't worked here long enough for the dread of this place to infect him just yet. He's young—younger than me—fresh out of college and has the excitement to learn like I once did. I don't want to have my negative thoughts infect him, so I try to put on a smile for a bit and engage in a bit of small talk.

"Oh, just got a lot on my mind. Don't worry about me, man. How are you liking the job?"

"So far it's great. I'm really liking working on the main line. All the crews have been so helpful, and I feel like I'm learning something new every day. Maintenance has also been a great help, offering a hand whenever they can."

I realize how different our perspectives of this place are. He works in the main line where everybody's attention is at. If he calls for resources, be it new equipment or staffing, he gets them with zero hesitation. If he needs help in making repairs or troubleshooting the line, there are people knowledgeable about the equipment that he can ask. But I'm stuck in the back of the plant, on an island all by myself knowing that I have nobody else to ask for help. Sometimes Cory will know the answer, but if he's not working or if he's stuck doing supervisor duties, then I'm on my own. What else is new?

"Good man. I'm glad. If you ever feel like switching departments, we could always use some more helping hands out by the saws."

"Oh, working in that disaster? No, I'm all right. I like where I'm at. I'm sure you wouldn't want my help anyway."

I got a bit angry at that remark. So, I reply, "Yeah, you're right. I wouldn't want your help. I'll be all right on my own. Good luck on your shift today. Don't get too dirty. I'm sure the managers wouldn't like that."

His expression changed like he knew he misspoke. He tries to save a bit of the conversation,

"Oh, sorry I didn't mean…"

"It's all right. I know you did."

I proceed to head out to the saws. "Just get through the day." That's all I care to think about. And so I do. I think, *I need time, time dedicated just to be able to dig deeper, to find the answers I desire.* My mind thinks of the possibilities. I caution myself not to do anything too rash, like quit my job immediately, even though it is enticing. I know the responsibilities that tie me down, most being financial. But I know I have done well so far in staying ahead of those, and it may have granted me the timeframe in which I will be able to find what I am looking for. A vacation, that's what I settle on, but to a place I have never been, a place where I have no expectations. It seems as any place is viable as I don't usually travel or care to. I felt like I never deserved it, like I didn't work hard enough…not enough…I want to dive into that feeling every time I say those words. They have gripped me. But I move my focus towards the present question, "Where should I go?" Hawaii. That is the place that pops up in my head. There is no real rhyme or reason. It was merely the first thing that came to mind.

How do I get there? Where do I stay? How long should I stay? How long can I stay? Many more questions pop up, but they don't really matter. My mind just wants to stay tied to the recent discovery. Hawaii, the more I say it to myself, the more I feel like manifesting it into this world. Before the day is over, I head back to the office and print out vacation request forms with so much excitement, for it feels like the first true step in this path. When do I want to go, or rather when can I go? So I head to the manager's office and look around for him. He's a heavyset figure around the same height as me. He shaves his head as he is balding on the top, so he makes sure it looks cohesive. He sports a goatee that covers most of his lower jaw and helps hide his slight double-chin. He has a limp when he walks because of old injuries from his contract with the army. He usually wears normal crew tees with some sport memorabilia (He's a Cowboys fan). His office also displays a lot of his sports memorabilia to further demonstrate his loyalty to his team. He has a soft-spoken demeanor and can be easily be approached. He does carry a lot of pride from his military days but also keeps his sociable demeanor by being the jokester in the front offices.

He is sitting down, and he sees me.

"Hey, Keith—"

Before I can say anything more, he abruptly interrupts, "What's up, sunshine? I was actually just looking for you. I got some good news."

"Oh, really? What is it?"

"Remember the director of R&D?"

"Yeah, that short Asian guy, right? What about him?"

"Well, he was impressed at how the saws ran when he was here and is looking to buy more of those machines for the plant, for some newer products he's looking to make. We're looking to get some more installed by the end of the year."

I don't know how he sees that as good news. I can barely handle two machines, and the company wants to throw another one on my lap to try and run. I've learned to bite my tongue enough and just accept the punishment.

"Yeah, that's awesome. Would you think I'd have time to be able to take a week off before the new machines get here?"

"Yeah, of course. We got Cory here. He can manage without you for a week."

"Oh, ok. Great. When will be the best time to do so?"

He replies, "Don't worry about when. Just take it off whenever you want."

It made me feel as if he understood the reasons why. Out of all the managers in the plant, he was seen to be the one most active on the floor and seeing the day-to-day problems. He's seen the sweat and the blood on the floor. He respected me enough to not say anything more.

"Thanks, boss. Let me get with Cory to see his schedule, and I'll get back to you."

"Sounds good, man."

I immediately head back to the plant and talk to Cory. He sees me approach him and says, "What's up, sunshine?"

"Not much, Cory. So, you want the bad news or the worse news?"

"What's that? I guess I'll take the worse news."

"We're getting another saw."

"Oof, yeah, that is some bad news. When do they want to install it?"

"By the end of the year."

"Great. What's the bad news?"

"I'm taking a week off."

"Oh, that's not bad at all. If there's anybody here who needs it, it's you. They got you by the balls working like crazy with these machines."

"Yeah, I know. And it's only going to get worse with that new machine on the way. I was going to ask you what your summer schedule was like so I know when I can take the time off and still have coverage for the saws."

"I appreciate that. Me and my family take a few weeks off in July to go fishing, but the rest of the summer is pretty open."

"Sound's good, Cory. I'll shoot for some time in June then."

I get some work done and make sure to head back to my manager's office to make sure he's aware of the days of my vacation.

"Hey, Keith. I talked to Cory. Looks like he's going to be taking some time off in July, so I'll plan for earlier. You think I can take the week of June twenty-first off?"

"Yeah, sure. I'll write it down on the calendar."

It's March. Why did I choose a week so far out? Because I have to feel like I've earned it, like I've worked far enough ahead to merit a week off. Eight weeks seems like enough time. The day is over, and I head home to start planning. I look at my bank account, and the tickets for the trip. I start trying to allocate as many funds as possible to be able to buy the tickets. I see the price for the tickets and hesitate a bit thinking, *Can I use this money for something else? Maybe I should keep it in the savings account. Maybe I should invest this money. Stop. Just stop and get the tickets before you talk yourself out of it.* So I buy the tickets hastily to ensure I don't lose out on the moment. June 19th is the day the flight leaves, on Father's Day.

Dad, there's much I want to tell you and Mom. I remember how much you and Mom have done for all of us. It brings me back to the times when you took us to visit your roots and the family you both had left behind many years ago. That place left a permanent mark in my mind.

Maybe I should have chosen that spot, that small town in Mexico and visit all the aunts and uncles down there. I want to, but I don't think that's the right place or time to go. I don't know if I'm ready to see the rest of my family disappointed at me. They all probably think I'm doing ok. I mean I'm in the US and should have no problems. I don't have to worry about my next meal or trying to pay the bills on time. I don't want to go there defeated when I have been given more to succeed. I want to explore a new place, hoping it brings with it new answers. I've heard much of the same sentiment from my family, "Just keep working through it. Just keep working no matter how bad it gets." I don't want to hear all the same words only rephrased by my aunts and uncles. I'll stick to the original plan.

As the days continue to pass, I remind myself to stay strong until the 19th, for the days continue to be long and grueling. My body has grown leaner day to day, and I have noticed it. It is partly because of the lack of nutrition from me not eating at work and barely having the motivation to eat when I get home. I find it hard to be able to continue to move and work with food sitting in my stomach. I try to make sure to eat simpler foods, like fruit and fruit snacks because it is the only thing my stomach is able to handle. The constant pit in my stomach from the anxiety causes me to not want to eat much else. Force-feeding food is the only way I can eat, and it leaves me a bit weary and my soul a bit deflated, thinking it is a struggle just to eat some food. Sometimes, I'll be able to work up an appetite after a while but only after a heavy day of weight training. I still try to keep the work output high, especially physically. I don't intend to stop these physical pursuits, not now, not ever. Not until my bones have become frail and my muscles have shriveled into raisins.

Physical pursuits. What do they mean to me? Why do I always feel the need to move, to push my body? These passing days have allowed me the mental focus to answer this for myself. They have concentrated this discipline into a forging of a strong mind. They inherently have no rules, for I am free to explore the limits of my body. My hands have grown rough, like sandpaper, from all the punishment they have endured. They have been callused, as the rest of my body has been. My body has hardened itself through this process, over and over again. The additional muscle is a nice result of this process, but I forewent that as the reason to continue these pursuits a long time ago. The bar, the weights, my body, they have all been there for me as able soldiers and confidants for the battles against every ounce of disdain, despair, depression, and anxiety. They have been there to help quell that overwhelming pit in my soul and have grown me to be the person I am today. My body is a reflection of the diligence, the discipline, and the motivation to progress. I dove deeper into these pursuits recently as I believe I have stagnated everywhere else in my life. Mentally, I feel like I have grown feeble. Emotionally, I have been unbalanced for so long that I have lost touch with many emotions. Spiritually, my soul has grown a bigger void, and I feel like I have grown deaf to God's words. But my body, it can still progress. It has allowed me to continue moving forward and has shown me the true depths to which I am able to go. And when I had nothing left to give, my pride fueled me, even going so far as sacrificing my own well-being, almost breaking my bones, my tendons, to be able to progress even an inch or an ounce. And after that breaking point at the beach, I have come to realize that although my soul was the one to fuel me, my body was the one to follow those commands diligently. And after all the pain I have put it through I must commend it:

My body, my willing-and-able soldier. You have been by my side through all of the ups and downs. You have never faltered. Even though at times you have felt subpar or even broken, we have found a way to persevere. You have helped me carry all of my sorrows, all of my pains, and all of my insecurities, and have done so with no hesitation. We have grown in the life together. At youth, we were both weak, naïve, but also innocent. We both could handle the growing pains, and there wasn't much we hesitated to do, at least in the sense of physical barriers. As we have matured together, we have honed in on the few activities we will pursue till the day we die. These activities have sharpened us. Every day we have carved the sculpture. We have chiseled a bit out one day at a time. We have both realized that there are many more battles ahead. Some will be physical; some will be mental. But we will ride alongside each other in battle.

I am sorry for abusing you during times of distress. I am sorry for trying to put extra pressures of fixing my internal issues through you. In many of my adult years. You have been my only friend, the only one to fully understand my mind. You have accepted of all the punishment, sometimes even excess punishment as well. I have pushed you to your limits time and time again, and still you have not given up on me. You are the only physical tool that God gave me to pursue my purpose in this life. You have earned the right to rest, but now, for now at least, there is no time to rest. We have many tasks ahead. Our journey will last this lifetime, and when the day comes when God judges me, I hope I can have these words to describe your efforts as well so that you can access all the rest you need. For at that time, our journey will be finished. Until that day comes, we must continue this path. I will commit to you, my sword, my body. I will provide for you the sustenance. I will provide for you an environment that will suit you as best as possible. I have started to see the signs of cracks, and it is time to mend them now. We must be ready for the ensuing battles. You are my best friend, my most willing-and-able soldier, and I will learn to love you again. I am sorry it took me so long for me to realize this, but please, just be patient a little while longer, for you will find peace soon.

These two hands are the only two things I have in this world to be able to manifest my dream. My dream, once I knew what it felt like to have one, and I have since lost it. But that day at the beach has somehow been able to spark that drive to find a new one for myself. What depths the soul can sink into without such a piece to hold on to my hope. Without it, it seems I have become hollow. I want to do justice to my soul and my body. I want to create that environment to be able to grow again. What is creating that drift in my spirit? What has caused me to fall so low? I need to find the source of these issues.

The days continue to pass, and longer and longer they seem, as June 19th approaches. I want nothing else but to make it to that day. My body has been actively wanting that break it deserves. My mind wants that escape from this daily prison. My soul wants to feel the life of fresh air, in a place that can embrace me with no preconceptions, no prejudice of character, and no expectations. Expectations, something I have given myself too much of. So in response to these dragging days, I have tried to find excitement in the small inconsistencies, the ones that previously irritated me. My mind has become efficient at so many tasks at work that they have dulled my senses even more. My body has also been accustomed to the workload and finds for more challenges to be able to feel satisfied, even though it grows weary. Days after work, I am able to find a bit more excitement to head to judo training, as it helps pass the time so I don't have to think about the remaining time until the vacation.

During the training, I find myself running with my head held a little higher and with my stride covering more ground. My body feels lighter, and I feel more present. All because I have something to look forward to in the near future. Part of me wishes to feel like this all the time, to embrace this, but I know that is not how I am. I have learned to embrace chaos. But today, I will relegate the mystery for a later date, for the analysis of my soul will be one journey that will take more of me than anything else. During training, I am usually the one to get picked for demonstrations or partner work. I guess I am good at taking the beating. Judo is a heavy sport at times. It uses many throws and takedowns and it leaves the body feeling drained. There have been countless times that I have been thrown with full force, luckily unscathed except for the bumps and bruises. Wearing a gi makes all the exercise more demanding as it allows for even more sweat to pour out of my body. After a good training session, my shoulders find it difficult to lift my arms and keep my head high. My hair is full of sweat, and my hands feel numb. At times, I wish to feel that exhaustion to hide many feelings and to just get down to a state of being that only thinks of sustenance and rest. Other times, I wish to feel that for pride, as a reminder as how deep the wells are of my potential.

Today, I am partnered with another senpai. She is about my size with curly blond hair. She carries a smile that is infectious and is a person who likes to brighten up the room. Her eyes are an inviting shade of blue, and they leave the door to her soul open as if saying she has nothing to hide in this world. She has been a person I admire for one simple reason: even though this world has been full of much corruption and sin, she has been able to grow without faltering in her faith and is able to keep both her innocence and purity. She is a truly unique and rare soul in this world and a valued friend, or at least I see her as a friend.

We begin our drills and simple small talk ensues, but nothing of substance comes out of it. She then notes, "You look tired."

I draw a blank. I feel like I should have been able to come up with a response quickly, but I am left speechless. Another person who recognizes the wearing of my body and soul. It feels like I take too long to respond, and so I go on with the first thing that comes to mind. "How'd you notice?"

"The bags under your eyes are getting pretty deep, and your techniques don't feel as consistent as they normally do."

How long has this been noticeable? I don't want to ask in fear of having the answer be longer than what I would like to hear. So in order to salvage a bit of the remaining pride, I respond,

"Well, soon I'll be able to take a break. I'll be heading on vacation in a few weeks."

"Oh cool, where you heading?"

"Hawaii."

"Sweet! Dude, I hope you have a good time. You deserve it."

Do I really deserve it? I don't know why that was the first thought that popped in my head. What do I deserve in this world? What does God intend for me to accomplish in this world? I'll have time to deconstruct these thoughts soon enough.

The practice finishes, and per the usual, I am drained. Another day filled with much work finished but with much more left on the table. I stay a bit after practice, and I decide to stick around and chat with the group. It's because I am too tired to move to my truck, and I hope that starting up a conversation or two will engage my mind enough to be able to get home. I sit down on the benches overlookng the mats, all drenched in sweat and just glancing at the room. The judoka who was my partner decides to stay too, and we talk. She asks how I am.

"I'm tired. Too much of the same bullshit on the daily is just wearing on me."

"Yeah, I didn't want to say anything, but I've noticed you're a bit leaner now, too. Have you been eating?"

"I eat when I can. I just don't want to be weighed down by a heavy meal if I'm stuck moving around all day at work."

"Yeah, I can see your point. How's everything else going on in your life?"

"I mean, you're looking at it. Not much else I got going on besides this and work."

"Have you thought about picking up other hobbies or looking for somebody?"

"No. Honestly, it seems like those things are a bit out of reach at the moment."

"Yeah, I can see that. Have you talked to work about giving you a better schedule?"

"No, they're not ones to budge when it comes to that stuff. Product has to ship by Friday is their mentality."

I see myself divulging more information than I normally would, partly because I am tired enough to allow these feelings to flow out of me. But there is a bit of me that finds her trustworthy as I see a good-hearted person in front of me. And because of this I don't want to leave a sour taste in her mouth and ruin her mood so I decide to change topics.

"Sorry, I don't mean to bring you down. How've you been though?"

"No, that's fine. I don't mind. I'm always here to listen whenever you need somebody. But things are good. My husband and I are heading out to vacation ourselves soon, too."

"Oh, that's great. Where are you guys going?"

"We'll be heading to Cancun for our honeymoon!"

"Dude, that's exciting. How long have you been married?"

"We've been married for about a year now."

"Oh, so why so late of a honeymoon?"

"We couldn't afford it at the time, but we finally were able to save up for the trip we wanted."

That little bit of joy in her eyes filled me with a bit, too.

"That's so awesome. I hope you have a great time. Make sure you have a few drinks for me while you're there."

"Thanks. I'm sure you'll be having enough for yourself down there in Hawaii!"

"Oddly enough, I don't drink. I haven't since my college days."

"Really? What for?"

It is a bit personal. It reminds me of an old story with my uncle. One I wish not to detail, but I see her inviting eyes and it makes me give in a little bit. I can't hold back all these memories anymore.

"Well, my family has had issues with drinking problems. My parents are responsible, but my family in Mexico is where the trouble is at. Every time I see a bottle, it just brings me back to a vivid image I have of my uncle, and... yeah."

The image of my dad's brother, my uncle Paco, fills my mind as I say those words and halt any more words that I was going to say. It's a vivid memory, one I don't realize I have compartmentalized for so long. I remember my uncle, just sitting down, defeated in a rundown room. He is sitting on a broken bed with his shoulders hunched forward. It's like he couldn't raise his head any higher as shame buried his spirit long ago and is just waiting for his body to give up.

"Oh, I see. You don't have to share more. I understand."

"Thanks. I appreciate you listening. You didn't have to."

"It's all right. Thank you for sharing. I know it's not easy sometimes."

"Agreed."

It seemed like it was the first person I talked to about anything of substance for a long time, and it probably was. I noted that she had no judgement or scorn or malice, or even a sense of interjecting between comments. She merely listened. I felt heard, for the first time in a long time, it was such a foreign feeling to me. And I wish to emulate that trait from her. My mind has grown comfortable around her, and my soul feels more at ease for knowing somebody is there to listen. Maybe that vacation will help unlock those secrets for me.

The weeks come and go slower and slower as the anticipation to leave that day grows inside of me. I try to hold that feeling at bay and not think about anything else but the present moment in the hopes of time ticking faster, but it doesn't help. One more week, that's all I need to endure. To try and fill the weekend, I work on some chores around the house, and it helps distract me slightly from the constant feeling of wanting to leave.

I think about what else I'll need to do in order to get to Hawaii. What do I need to pack? Who's going to take care of the house? Should I take a day off to help prepare? How do I get to the airport? All are simple questions, and they seem easy enough to answer. The airport is a few hours away and that will be the hardest thing to try and arrange. I don't know of many people who'd be willing to drive six hours just to take me to the airport. So I decide to ask my parents as a last resort. I have felt so busy that I let myself lose focus and I forgot to try and call my mom again. I realize I haven't made the time to even visit them in a long time, even though they live only an hour away. My life has drifted from them in many ways, not just physically but emotionally as well. I left their nest a long time ago, and every day apart from them seems to grow that disconnect even more. Ever since I left home, I have always felt an unnerving pressure from them, one that is hard to describe. And there is no real tension between us besides that one artificially created in my mind. It makes it hard to ask them, but I have to in order to get to Hawaii. So I corral the courage to pick up the phone and dial what was once home.

As the phone rings, I find myself a bit nervous waiting to hear my dad on the other line. Each ring of the phone makes me want to hang up and find a different way to get to the airport. My heart seems to fill the resounding silence in the room from its excessive beating. And it wants me to move from my seat, but my body won't move an inch, not because it doesn't want to, but because this pressure won't allow me to.

Then finally, I hear, "Hey, son. What a miracle! You actually called."

I instantly gain my composure, as if my dad's words triggered this from me. I need to show to him that I'm doing ok, so he doesn't worry. I don't want to have him stress over me and how I'm really doing. "Hey, Dad, sorry for not calling more often. Just been busy with work. How are you?"

"No worries, son. I understand. And you know, just dealing with your mother and her projects. She doesn't let me rest much."

"Yeah, I know how she gets. She's one to always stay busy."

"Yeah. You know Father's Day is coming up, it's this Sunday. Me and your mom want to make a carne asada at our house. You're going to make it right?"

"No, Dad, I don't think I'll be able to make it. I'm actually going on vacation and leaving this weekend."

"Oh, is that right? Where are you going?"

"Hawaii."

"Oh, wow. So who's going to take care of the house?"

"I'll ask the neighbors to watch it for me. It should be simple enough. But I wanted to call because my flight leaves out of Sacramento since it's cheaper to fly out from there, so I need somebody to drive me that Friday night. I know this is kind of short notice, but do you think you can give me a ride, Dad?"

"Oh, it's not too late. I'd be happy to. Do you want your mom to come with us?"

"No, that's ok. I know she probably works that night, too."

"Oh ok. I'll let your mom know then. What time do you want me to pick you up? What time does your flight leave?"

"I'm leaving Saturday morning, eight AM, so I was thinking we can just book a hotel room for Friday night, so you can just drop me off at the airport on your way back home Saturday morning. You can pick me up whenever you can."

"Oh ok, I'll stop by after work then. Five PM sound ok?"

"Yeah, that's fine, Dad. I'll be ready by then. Thank you, Dad."

"No worries, mi hijo. I'll see you on Friday. I love you. Your mom does, too."

As he says those words, my eyes begin to tear and I lose my composure. So I steadfastly say, "Love you too, Dad." And I hang up right after. Those words, the ones that help build one's soul, they managed to do the opposite to me.

I just sit here, in this blank kitchen, surrounded by these plain white walls, and look down at my phone. I see tears covering the surface of it. *Where are they coming from? From me, but how? Maybe I'm just tired.*

The voice from my heart chimes in, "Stop lying to yourself. You're not just tired. You're breaking like I've been trying to tell you. Open your eyes for once. How much more do you have left? How much longer can you go living like this?"

"I don't know"

Those words weigh me down for the rest of the day. I cannot hide or run away from the fact that they are true. Is that why it hurt so badly because I finally stopped lying to myself about how I really was? Probably. I have no place to hide, especially from myself. So what's the point in running from this anymore? I can't even get through a conversation with my parents without crying right after. It's pathetic, it really is. Pathetic. I thought the floor to the well of my sorrows had already been reached, but there are even greater depths to this. I get a sudden reminder of the beach, as if the connection it has to these sorrows helps bring forth this memory. Those feelings that I had felt that day also start to fill my heart. That pity I felt for myself back then is present. That shame, that disappointment, all of it hits me again. The sound of the tide forms in my ear calling me to come back as its songs are so soothing. I see the ocean surface and the starry night sky as the scene looks as appealing as the first time. The feeling of warm winds and the soft sand cover my skin again, caressing me as they did that night. But my soul is not blind to any of this anymore. It knows of the false promises this place holds. And these bodily sensations don't persist as long or penetrate as deep, but they are there serving as a reminder to how weak my character has become and how far that lighthouse really is. That shining glimmer of hope is focused on getting through this week. Just one more week and I'll be able to start finding peace.

The day comes to a close, and I head upstairs for the night as the week begins anew tomorrow. The house seems eerily empty and the air still. My senses have been on high alert ever since the call with my dad, and so it perceives things much more vividly. The same environment I come home to every night and wake up to every day seems to catch my attention more. I live in a midsize townhome in the outskirts of the main city. It's a two-story house with an exterior mix of a beige and dark brick. Its color scheme was set to match the other houses on the lot. They all look the same with only a few standout features in each.

It's a good size for a townhome, much more than what a single person would ever need, having three bedrooms upstairs and the main living quarters downstairs. What covers the bottom floor is a light grey laminate—smoked oak is what the builders called it—surrounded by nothing but matte white walls, exactly the same as the ceiling in my room. The bottom floor is an open living space with no distinct end or start to the kitchen and living room. The kitchen has the only contrast to this whole house it seems, with tall white bar-style granite countertop. The cabinets are all colored with a dark wood stain, something akin to an espresso. All the appliances are stainless steel creating a modern look. I added some light furniture to the main living quarters. Seeing as I don't spend much time here, it didn't merit me dressing it up too much. I have a small square dinner table that was gifted to me by my mom upon renting the first place away from my parents' home years ago. Its wood color matches the cabinetry well and has a modern look to it, too. I also have a few barstools that help give me another option for guests by the granite countertops. I use these to sit most of the time when reading emails or just having a quick meal before bed. It's a nice place, but it's bland with no real flavor.

I feel synonymous to this place. It mirrors my inner being well, almost too well. I don't like staying at this house often as I find the time alone constraining. This place actively holds a mirror to myself and shows me just how unidimensional I have become. I feel as if I could stand next to a wall and blend right in. Weekends are when I spend the most time here, and it's almost unbearable. I want to spend time away from here, for although it is my house, it is not my home. I try to fill this time with activities away from this place for those reasons. And because of this, I find myself taking extra time at the grocery store or at the coffee shop or just driving.

In recent memory, I've found myself driving in any direction for an hour or two. I didn't care where I ended up, I just did not want to be here encased by these walls. I usually did not gain much or find much from these little miniature adventures, if it's right to even call them that, besides just killing the time. However, there was one place that seemed to resonate with me. It's an hour north of my house. A place right off the highway. Many people pass by it without noticing its beauty. I stumbled across it once, the summer I bought this house. The feeling of nothingness was even greater back then as I had nothing in this house besides the walls and cabinets. So I decided to leave for a few hours one day and found this place.

It's a foothill surrounded by the high and dry Nevada mountains to the east and the luscious green California mountains to the west. The dichotomy of the two regions splits right at this small river stream that follows the highway. The stream is surrounded by about ten-foot walls on both sides making it look like it has carved its place in the ground after years and years of constant flowing. When there is no traffic, the river can be heard as clear as day and provides a natural melody that soothes my soul. The California side of the foothills gradually climbs up to the mountaintops. It's covered with a consistent coat of green grass and shrubs all the way to the top. Nevada's side shows much more character as the foothills end abruptly and are taken over by steeper climbs and a more rigid texture. Sagebrush is the only thing to cover these mountains and sparingly at best. During the sunset, the California mountains disperse the light as one would think an angel has just left our presence. The bright color of the sun gradually turns into a subtle orange glow that accentuates the mountain's silhouette. When the moon takes its place, it typically resides with the eastern mountains also providing the chance for the Nevada terrain to glow and its silhouette to show. The stars can all be seen in full effect with no city lights drowning out the night sky. I want to go there again to say hi to all those stars in the skies once more. So I decide to take the truck and head north.

The drive is quiet. There are only a few cars on the road, and the highway seems to narrow the farther north I travel. The oncoming traffic lights remind me of the lighthouse, as they pass by in a similar rhythm. My mind grows lax behind the wheel, and it perceives the headlights as the lighthouse manifesting in front of me. My heart fills my body with a slight urge to pull the truck into it, and that thought in my head from the beach returns.

My heart intervenes, "Why not? You're that close to paradise. This time with less effort, just a slight tilt of the wheel, and we can make it. You know you're tired, and the lighthouse is passing us over and over again."

Will this voice always persist within me? I try not to entertain this plea much, but it festers. I can see through the deception this time around, but it grows after every car that passes. I make it to that place, finally and breathe a sigh of relief. It's night time by the time I make it. The sky is illuminated by an almost full moon. It seems brighter than usual and actually drowns out a few of the dimmer stars in the sky. I sit on top of my truck and just try to feel the environment. The wind passes in small gusts and excites the sagebrush to the left of me, calling out as if excited to see me. The river hums a beautiful melody that gets interrupted sporadically from the passing cars but still is able to soothe my soul even slightly. I look up at the stars and merely admire them for a moment. How I wish to be one of them.

As I look up, I become slightly jealous. It is not directed towards any person, but at the stars above, for they are free. They have all the space they desire between them, allowing for them to dance around the sky. They can grow as big or as small as they want and can shine their light the same. They can form their light to shine whatever color they can imagine. Their lives are formed so peacefully and their substance carries life across the multiple planets that are somehow present in the empty voids in the night sky. They are so beautiful that they attract other beings, planets, meteors, to dance around them. But most importantly, they are pure. They are untouchable to any corruption in this world. There is no such thing as sins, mistakes, or falsities for them. They are not bound by any dream or wish for they crave nothing more but to fill the night sky with their uniqueness. How I wish to be like them, to not be bound by these earthly tethers, to not be bound by the persistent soul. A soul that constantly pulls me back from peace in order to create something in this world. Maybe one day this soul can build a light bright enough to rival the stars. The time passes much faster here it seems, and it's time to head home to finish off this last week of work before vacation. If the stars look this beautiful out here, I wonder how beautiful they'll look down in Hawaii. I guess I'll find out soon enough.

Roots

FOUR AM, THE ALARM RINGS. My body wakes up with vigor. I don't remember how much rest I actually got last night, but it doesn't seem to matter. My body is already awake and ready to move. It's still dark outside, but the moonlight sparks my mind and makes me cognizant much faster than normal. I am present and in the moment. I know why. It's because it's the last day of work before I leave to Hawaii. I finally made it to Friday, and now I just need to get through one shift, and I'll have made it to temporary freedom. This anticipation is going to make the day drag much slower than I'd like. *Just strap these boots on, and get to work. Try not to think about the end of the day. We haven't made it yet.* Reciting this helps calm down that excitement in my heart just slightly and gets me composed to get ready and head over to work.

I step outside and smell a bit of freshness in the air. The stars are a bit visible when I look straight up and highlight the bright crescent moon. I wish I were able to sit down and see these stars until the sun comes up and they disappear for the day, but I'll be late for work. No matter, I'll make up for this. I'm sure of it.

The drive to work is calming as I drive east with less traffic than normal, and it gives me a front row seat to the sunrise. The light rises from behind the mountain range and illuminates the horizon with a golden amber. The mountains help block the brightness to allow for my eyes to see the purity of this color as it fades to a light blue. Usually, my mind is flooded with many memories or thoughts along this route, and it makes this scene look much blander. This morning not a single thought passes through my mind throughout the drive. Is this what peace feels like? My mind sets back into reality, or rather the dystopian life I see, but it doesn't seem as gloomy after viewing the sky change from the starry night to the serene sunrise. I get out of the car, and my shoulders don't feel as stiff, and my legs don't feel as weak. If only more days could feel like this. That excitement for the vacation to start helps carries the weight of the dull day.

The morning tasks seem to fly by as I try to get everything done as soon as possible to give me a good chance of leaving early. I tell the crew leads that I plan on leaving early and don't bother telling the managers as they all leave early on Fridays anyways. Many engineers follow suit and leave early, with only a few staying past 2PM. Ever since I started, I was relegated to staying late because the managers scheduled long production runs starting on Friday. There have been many days where I would work ten-, twelve-, even fifteen-hour shifts while I see everyone else able to leave after only six or seven hours. I resented them a bit, and it hasn't helped me feel like "part of the team" as if I ever really was. So today I will be a bit selfish and take an early day. I'll gladly accept any consequence from this. After the first few hours of the shift, time ticks slower and slower. I don't have any motivation to finish any more daily tasks, so I relegate my efforts to killing time. I head up front to the main offices sporadically throughout the day, more than usual, just to see when the managers decide to leave. Every time I do, I notice one fewer car in the parking lot. Each walk back out to the plant floor is slower as I make sure each sequence takes more and more time. After a few more cycles of this, I finally head back up front and see all the managers' cars have left the parking lot. I do a quick inspection of the front offices to make sure they are all truly gone, and they are. So I head to my desk, grab my bag, and head out, finally.

I breathe a big sigh of relief for making it this far. I get to my truck and turn off my phone to make sure I don't get any calls or texts from work. Finally, I get home and double check that I have everything I need for the trip. I double check my bags, my flight information, my passports, etc. I've done this so many times at this point, but one more time doesn't hurt. Now it's just a waiting game until my dad gets here. I give him a call to let him know that I'm home, but he doesn't answer or call back until he's off. I have time to myself, and it feels odd, but calming at the same time. A reassuring feeling grows the more I wait, saying that this was indeed the right decision. It helps quell some of the anxiety in my stomach. "How lucky am I, a small-town Hispanic kid, to make it to a place that some people may never get to visit in their lives. God, thank you."

"God, you've given me so much in this world. I have a roof over my head, a way to provide food on the table, and a means to make a living. Thank you for allowing this, but there is one thing I still must ask of you. I just ask for peace, for my soul and my mind, for my heart and my body. I wish to not have these pieces of me conflicting all the time. I know this is selfish of me to ask, but please, if there was one thing I could wish for, or pray for, that would be it."

I tear up a bit, not out of shame or fear, but out of happiness as the ambiance in my room fills with a comforting warmth that comes directly from the sun, and inherently from God himself. I feel like His hand is over my shoulder like a father sharing a special moment with his child. Finally, my dad calls me letting me know that he is right outside. That usual anxiety I have when seeing my parents is gone, maybe just momentarily, but I feel that moment with God helped me quell it, as if saying that it is my father's turn to share that moment with me.

"Hey, mi hijo."

"Hey, Dad."

"You ready to leave? You got everything?"

"Yeah, I'm all good to go. Let's get on the road."

We start our drive to California, and it's a bit quiet for the first few minutes. I'm not sure what to say, and I don't feel like talking about anything trivial. For my entire life, I have put my parents on pedestals in my mind. They have done so much in their lives and have built themselves up from nothing. My mom and my dad met in Mexico in a small town with not a lot of resources. They struggled a lot back then both from a young age. They both worked to get to college back in Mexico, something that was scarce during those times, and were able to get stable jobs right out of college. They could have lived a comfortable life close to their families. But they both were struck with the dream of an even greater life. They sacrificed the comfort of their environment and took a chance to make it to the land of dreams. My dad left first, on his own accord and started as a janitor in a place where his uncle worked. He was fortunate to have the opportunity. After some time, he gained the courage to call my mother and ask for her hand in marriage. She still lived in Mexico at the time, wondering where he was, but she agreed.

Their dreams matched along with their hearts and so they got married, and soon after she followed suit and left for the United States as well. From there, it was a typical story of immigrants making a living for themselves. They migrated to Nevada and found success in different careers. They both contained their struggles as they worked and learned more about the new country.

The town my parents grew up in was right outside of a major industrial city, maybe a couple bus rides to the city center. It is a dry and flat part of Mexico with very hot summers and warm winters. Rain and snow happen once in a blue moon. There is little vegetation besides a few one-off trees on the sidewalks and playgrounds. One thing that everybody has to be aware of are the scorpions, as they run rampant in that area. Waking up, people shake their shoes to make sure there aren't any hiding. Most, if not all, of the houses are made of brick and single story with lower roofs, maybe twelve feet at the highest. The lots did not have much room for a backyard, and if a house had a driveway, it seemed like a symbol of status. They all had a similar build and style, but each house had a distinct layout which provided them with variety, making each house distinct and one of a kind. The infrastructure seemed like it was properly done at one point around all the residential roads, but the lack of upkeep makes drives around the neighborhood an off-roading experience. Only the main highways and roads with heavy traffic were maintained, but only slightly. The paint denoting different lanes has faded and still has yet to be replaced. Safe to say that driving there is a thrill ride in and of itself. The people residing there lived humble lives, and the place reflects that because they molded it to be that way. They find unique ways to make it day by day.

Many people would, and still do, make small shops in their houses and sell simple groceries or snacks to the neighbors. Neighborhood kids go just around the corner to get their favorite snacks with little regard for safety. The town is small enough to know everybody so that helps curtail any crime and they all have a sixth sense in being able to determine when things seem to escalate. They all know the talk of the town and know how to stay out of any trouble because of it. Other people, mainly men, have normal nine-to-five-style jobs in the main city and work industry jobs. Come to think of it, that's probably how my family got so caught up in the work here in the States. After work, some families who own small food trucks would set up shop around the town around the evening hours. Those were the times when the heat would subside and the ambiance was much more suited to conversation. It seemed like that was the time that the town became alive. People lived simple lives back then and even now. And to think that my parents decided to forego that peace and home for something greater, for a chance to change the history of their family. Thinking about it makes me want to tear up. I lose sight of this a lot, as the daily tasks and constant inner dialogue make me cover up how far my roots actually go, but during these moments, I always gain more appreciation for my parents, and added motivation to keep moving forward.

I knew my parents were driven and focused, but it never hit me until they took me to their childhood homes when I was a teen. That's when the awe of them really sank in. To be able to see their humble beginnings to where they are now in life made me feel a sense of duty to them, one that could only be fulfilled by soaring to greater heights than them. It was only natural to think like this because of where I started. "If they can make it this far in life from where they started, then it would be a shame if I made it any less than them." Those have always been my thoughts towards them ever since I knew just how amazing they truly were. They never intended for me to see them that way, but I did. And ever since I was a young boy, I've been trying to make them proud, to earn their respect, even though they have told me countless times that I have, but I still cannot accept it. This only grew the rift between me and my family, but when and why did my roots begin to grow apart from theirs?

At ten years old, I remember telling my mother that I was done with birthday parties.

"Mijo, are you sure you don't want a birthday party this year?"

"Yeah, Mom. I'm sure. I don't think many people would show up anyways."

"We can invite some of our friends. They would love to come."

"Mom, its ok. I just don't want one this year."

"Me and your dad just want to make sure you have a good birthday. Is there anything you want for your birthday instead?"

"No, Mom. I'm ok."

"Ok, mijo."

I can still picture the strange look on my parent's faces. Back then, they weren't really sure how to react to it. They just wanted to give me the best celebration of the year, but I never felt like I was worth celebrating. I felt like this conversation repeated for a few years until my parents realized it was a futile effort. I'm sure that's when I started to grow apart, not just from my parents or siblings, but from everyone. Ever since that day, my heart felt malnourished of love, of friendship, of comradery. I was deaf to those calls so long ago and here it is now, screaming in my chest saying, "Please, just give me something to hold on to. Please just let me rest for a moment. I can't keep going like this. Please." It screams so loud that it drove me to almost take my life. How far have I truly fallen?

Ever since I was young, I have been aware, maybe not fully, but I have been able to see things in a different light. I could see the consequences of some of my actions and those of my siblings and even of others. My parents, as successful as they are, are not rich, and we learned how tight money could be whenever we made costly mistakes. I noticed the added stress we provided them, albeit unintentionally, when we made mistakes.

Our parents would come and be shocked. "Who broke the TV?"

I would respond to help take the blame away from my brother and sister. "Sorry, Mom, it was me."

"Why, mijo? We didn't just buy a TV for you to break it. Back in Mexico, your cousins don't even have TV to watch and here you are breaking it for no reason. Come on, mijo, you should know better."

"You're right, Mom. I'm sorry."

My mom would always hit us with this line to really make things sting, "If you were really sorry, you would have never done it."

I could barely stand hearing those words, so I tightened up. I learned to make minimal mistakes. I worked hard in school to make sure I got solid grades, As only. Bs meant I didn't work hard enough. I got lucky here since I was a quick learner. I made sure to stay in line in school and not cause any more problems outside of it. My parents tried to teach us many things, but mainly to be peaceful, to stay in control. Through the years, life picked up on that and bestowed upon me the "golden child" standard. My parents never placed this standard on me. It merely crept in from the years of trying to do my best and being a good son. External factors reinforced this standard on me. I slowly became an honors student and was the one my siblings were always compared to. They held a bit of hate in their hearts because of this, and I couldn't blame them. I never intended to make them feel that way, but I saw it as a consequence of my actions and I tried to drift away from them, too. I didn't want life to compare us. It's not right or fair to them or me. Even when I tried to do things right, they seemed to never end well.

The better I did at school, the more I would get picked on for not letting the popular kids prevail. They hazed me at times. I wouldn't go as far as to say bullied, but I did catch some heat because of my soft-spoken manner. Everybody knew I wouldn't fight back, so it gave some kids the greenlight to take advantage of that. I hated it, but I didn't want to cause a ruckus, so I took it without saying a word, even letting some kids cheat in the hopes of buying some freedom from the hazing. It didn't work well. It only made me feel like a run-down prostitute. They would always find new ways to keep the hazing coming and find ways to take what they needed from me to get through class with minimal effort. It ate me up inside. I wanted to fight back, but I didn't want to disappoint my parents.

That pain of being alone, of never being accepted, of trying to uphold a standard for myself, of being the golden child, it all festered inside of me. Reminiscing about it all makes me realize that my heart's intentions of taking me to that place makes more sense than I originally thought. I tried to relieve some of this bottled-up tension, but no matter where or when, I was reprimanded. I tried to find friends, but I couldn't fit in. I didn't speak enough Spanish to be considered part of the "Mexicans" but somehow was too Mexican to be part of any other friend group. As I grew, I tried to find a different approach to this, maybe find a girlfriend. Being shy didn't help much at all, but I still tried. I had courage somehow and went for the most popular girls in school. Maybe it was because I felt like life said they were out of my reach, and I wanted to prove that theory wrong. It wasn't.

I would write letters to some of the girls I felt the most attracted to. Most, if not all, never even responded. *Maybe I didn't try hard enough.* I didn't know when to quit and still don't, I guess. Valentine's Day was no exception. I recall an old story that seemed to stick with me all these years.

"Hey, Erica." She was the prettiest girl in high school, and we shared the same math class.

"Oh hey…" She looked like she was trying to remember my name but couldn't and broke eye contact.

"Hey, so I got bored in history class, and since its Valentine's Day, I decided just to give this to you. I hope you like it." It was a handmade card and inside I drew a nice heart with her name in it with a cool font.

"Oh. Thanks." She hid the letter in her textbook right after, almost like she didn't want people to notice. I picked up on that and just went straight to my seat, head down, defeated again. As the bell rang for class to end, I walked out and saw that letter in the trash. I didn't know I could have felt more deflated than that moment. It felt like every year since then something similar would happen, like getting stood up for homecoming or being denied as a date for prom. I would continue to try though, out of my hearts plea to find some kind of relief. It sucked up whatever confidence I had left growing up; resentment took its place. To this day, I haven't had the opportunity to share Valentine's Day with anybody. No New Year's kiss, no birthday wish, no love letters, or candlelit dinners. No matter how much my heart desired it, no matter how much I desired it, I couldn't make that happen and it is the greatest failure I have committed to my heart. "I'm sorry, my heart. You don't deserve this." Then my ego carried me forward again, "If nobody cared to see the value in me then fine, I'll work until they can't ignore it any longer."

I tried to replace that resentment with success, and although the challenge of becoming successful was invigorated in me, it left the second I gained it. I tried to replace it with money, and that never seemed to satisfy me, either. The items I bought with it only gave me temporary satisfaction. Nothing seemed to work. That resentment has made me rotten. I can barely see my reflection because I don't see me. I see a man, or rather a child acting as a man, who still hears his parents' voices telling him what to do. They don't deserve this, though. It's not their voice, just an imitation, a weak one created by an even weaker mind hoping to block himself from any consequences of his actions. It's time to reconcile, or at least start to do so. My dad is right next to me, and I haven't said a word to him at all. It's only been fifteen to twenty minutes, but it feels like an eternity, enough time to collect these thoughts and memories. And certainly enough time to think of something to say.

"It's a nice drive." I mean, I guess that works, could've been a bit smoother but here we are.

"Yeah, driving through the mountains is always nice. How are you, mijo?"

"I'm all right, Dad. Just a bit stressed with work." The usual excuse.

"Yeah, it's good you're taking a break. You've always worked hard, sometimes a little too hard. But me and your mom are really happy and proud of you. You've made it far in life."

It still leaves me a bit uneasy when he says it, but I appreciate his words and try my best to accept them.

"Thanks, Dad. I'm trying. Can I ask you something?"

"Yeah, son, of course."

"How come you never told us much about your life? I've always wanted to know how you grew up."

It's true that I did, first just out of curiosity, but seeing him and my mother age makes me want to know more about them while I still have the chance.

"Well, I never thought you or your siblings needed to know. It's not very interesting. I'm a lot like you, very reserved."

"Well, maybe I don't need to know, but I want to know."

"Ok. Well, what do you want to know?"

"How was grandpa? I know you never talked much besides him being a drunk? And I never really got a chance to meet him."

"Oh well, my dad…he was an interesting person."

"How so? Was he…violent?"

"Only when he drank, but he would drink a lot."

"Oh." I didn't want to ask anymore, but he went on with a story.

"Yeah, there was a time when I saw him get in a fight in the bar. He was on the floor getting beat up with a pool ball."

"Woah, really? Do you know why?"

"I think he said he was mad for losing too much money or not getting paid for a debt. I don't think it mattered. He was drunk. I think they both were."

"How did he make it out?"

"Well, I saw him get back up and starting beating up the other guy. He finished the fight, but I saw him with a bloody face and some cuts and scrapes all around his arms."

"Dad, you never told me this. Why?"

"I mean, you never really met him, so I didn't think I mattered too much. And you never asked."

"Yeah, I guess that makes sense. How old were you when this happened?"

"I think about ten."

Upon him retelling these stories, I notice something. He's stoic, stone cold, and he has no expression on his face. It's like he's reading a book of a stranger's life, as if he had no attachment to it. I pull a lot from that. As he says these things, I can't help but think that there are probably a dozen more stories that he can recount that would mirror this one. Life has shown him much, so nothing could shake his demeanor or his will, and I admire that. But it also saddens me a bit listening to it as I realize that being the responsible one probably forced him to not feel things.

"Dad, my whole life, the twenty-seven years I've been alive, I've never seen you cry, not once. "

"That's right."

We left it at that. Life showed him a lot, and he built his resolve while learning to accept the flaws and imperfections of his world. He's a reserved man, and now I know why, partly by nature and partly by environment. It has allowed him to process life at his own pace. We are not too dissimilar. He enjoys his solitude, as do I. I do understand the differences between us however. Where he is stoic and calm, I am more inclined to follow instinct and emotion. He knows and prefers to internalize matters of the heart and mind. Try as I might, I am unable to do so for they fester inside me for too long. Where he can be reserved, I need to express. His traumas have stemmed in life, and mine seem to stem in love. No matter our differences, there is one thing that resonates with me and I understand completely, and that's his relationship with his brothers.

"How's Tio (uncle) Paco doing?"

We both stopped for a moment, and he replied somberly, "The same."

"Oh…Dad, what made Tio Paco like that? How did he get to where he's at?"

That image of him in Mexico in that rundown room fills my mind. As I glance at my dad, his stoic face breaks character for a moment. He takes another moment to respond, as if trying to put that charade back on, and responds, "You know, your Tio Paco has always been really shy. He's never really had a lot of confidence in himself. Growing up, he wouldn't play much with us or the neighbors and he would just be inside watching me and my brothers play. We would try to invite him out but he never wanted to."

"This is going to be a long story isn't it, Dad?"

"Yeah, probably."

"Well, I'm all ears."

"Well, me and my siblings always tried to get him out of his shell, but he just didn't want to. He was always a bit heavier and bigger and I think that didn't help. He would get picked on every once in a while, and I remember my oldest brother—your Tio Jorge—would fight the kids who would pick on him. He never really had many friends. The friends he did have weren't really the best influences and he would let them take him to some parties when he got older."

"Is that where he picked up drinking?"

"A little bit but not too much. When I left home was when he started to drink a lot more."

"What happened, Dad?"

"Well, when I left for the US, I wanted to bring everybody up. I had my uncle here, and he was going to help bring my mom up to visit and the rest of my siblings, but your Tio Paco couldn't make it."

"Why couldn't he?"

"I tried to help get his visa in on time, but he couldn't get it. All of my other siblings had them from prior visits except Paco. I tried to get it done quicker and sent back to him, but I didn't have the money for the visa."

"So did he have a place to stay? How did he manage with all of you guys in the US at the time?"

"He stayed with my dad…and that's when he picked up drinking and smoking a lot."

My dad's face shifts as he continues on. His tone softens, and he becomes a bit more somber.

"I feel like it was my fault for not getting him here when I had the chance. I feel like I could have helped him not go down that path."

I know, and his siblings know, it wasn't his fault, but I understand the grief. If I could put it into my own words, it would be like having the ability to save a person from jumping from a cliff and not doing so. Even though it wasn't your fault or volition in putting them in that circumstance, you still have guilt of allowing it to happen. How long has this been eating him up inside? I remember my dad trying to make it up to Paco a few years later by bringing him up to the States for a while. My siblings and I were around during this time, and I vaguely remember his visit. We all didn't spend much time with him, but I grew to love him more and more. I felt like even during my younger years, I could feel the loneliness in his heart, and it resonated with me. Ever since that visit, whenever my dad would check up on his siblings, I would always ask to see how Paco was doing before anybody else. Knowing more of his backstory, and in essence his demise, only grows the sadness in my heart. That image of him in that dark room, where he presumably still resides, is much more vivid. It's like with this added information it fills the gaps of my memory.

The room was not much bigger than a twenty foot by twenty-foot floor space, if that. The brick wall was starting to fall apart and there are some holes that should've been patched months ago. The floor was once tile, but it has all eroded and turned to dry gravel now. His bed was a bit too small to hold his big frame, and it rested on top of a few bricks, probably the ones that fell from the wall. There was only one light in the center of the floor space, and it hung from the wiring. There was a small wash area, not a shower, but a place with a drain and a bucket where he bathed. Right next to that was a toilet which didn't seem to work and was permanently stained from the dirt in the air. Lying around the entire floor space were empty forty-ounce beer bottles. The smell was a mix between broken plumbing, car grease, and beer. His shirts were all hung up by a small wire that he hung up across his room; most of them were stained or had holes in them.

As I saw that with my own eyes, I finally understood what a broken man was, and to have him as a person I care for dearly, hit me hard. At the time I was speechless, but composed, probably because my dad accompanied me. I felt an unnerving amount of guilt and shame from this, like any form of complaining or ungratefulness was immediately reflected back on myself. And I knew that my dad's feelings seeing his brother like this must have hit him deeper than I could know. To this day, it has been the only story my father has told me that has showed his will falter.

As he is telling me these things, I immediately feel how he does, just not to the extent that he does. It makes me feel like I haven't been there for my siblings as much as I should have, like I've been a subpar brother.

"Dad?"

"Yeah, mijo?"

"Am I a bad person?"

"No, of course not. Why do you say that?"

"I don't talk to my siblings at all, and I barely talk to you guys. I feel like I'm not part of the family anymore, and it's nobody's fault but mine."

"Listen, mijo, we know that you are grown and that you want to live your own life. We want to spend time with you, but we know that life gets in the way. We'll always be here for you, and so will your siblings. We love you, and that's not going to change no matter what."

"Thanks, Dad. How's Carlos doing?" Carlos is my little brother. It's hard not to think about him after hearing the story my dad just told me. I don't keep up with him much, not since I left home. He's a spontaneous kid, one to always be the life of the party and needs to be out and about. He can't be stuck at home for long. Because of that, he has always been the one to find himself in troublesome predicaments.

"He's doing ok. He's still out partying a bit and trying to do too many things at once."

"Yeah? What's he doing for work now?"

"He's a bartender. He has a few bars he works at downtown."

"Oh. Is he drinking a lot, too?"

"Yeah…"

"Oh"

"Keep an eye on him, mijo, please."

"I will, Dad."

I feel like I'm listening to the same story repeat itself. I didn't know I was this out of touch with my own family. I want to text my brother right now to see how he's doing, but I didn't want it to feel forced. He's a bit abrasive at times and doesn't like to have people check up on him. "I'm not a baby anymore," is his usual response. It's hard to speak with him sometimes, and I can't show any concern or else he'll just stop talking all together. He's a good kid, though. He's slowly turning the corner, but he just wants to live a fast life, and I can't do anything but watch and be ready if he crashes. Man, that hurts just to think about.

As we talk, we pass the Sierra Mountains and are able to see Lake Tahoe at the peak of the drive. The trees hover over the lake in an effort to hide this treasure to only those who value its beauty. The sunlight glistens over the water with no clouds in sight allowing the lake to mimic the sky perfectly. The lake has calm still water, in perfect harmony with its home and it helps ease my soul. As the sun sets, the sky transforms into a golden amber that draped itself over the water and covered its surface with the same unique colors. I wish we had the time to stay to see the moonlight reflect off the water's surface. "That's a pretty sight, huh, Dad?"

"Yeah, it is, mi hijo. Your mom loves this view, too."

"Yeah, I like it a lot, too."

"You know, your mom has been worried about you?"

"Why?"

"You know how she is."

"Yeah, I do."

"You know your mom and I always say, through God we can handle anything."

"Yeah, I guess we'll find out."

I feel like my relationship with God has always been tumultuous. I feel close to Him at times, like this afternoon, but then I feel like I drift apart from Him and His words as time goes by. Life itself pushes and pulls me from Him, just as the moon does to the ocean waves. I feel like I am never on solid ground with God. I wish I was more like my mother in this sense, so convicted, so sure, and so faithful.

My mom is a beautiful person. She arguably has had a harder life than my dad, but her spirit has not faltered. My mom is one of eight siblings. She lived in the same town as my dad, but where my dad had means to make a living with the family businesses, my mom did not. Her father was a drunk and abusive and led to many nights of angst in her household. He had to care for nine other people by himself as my grandmother did not work. Money was always tight in the household, and she lived in a three-bedroom house that was much too small for a family half their size. My mom knew that she did not have many means to make a life after school, so she decided to drop out of school in her teen years to begin working. Her first job was in a sewing factory in which she lied about her age to be able to work there. They required everyone to by sixteen years or older. She was fourteen at the time.

Where my dad was given the title of the "responsible sibling," my mother took it for herself. My mom's good nature shined; even in her youth she was able to make good friends in any area in life. Her work ethic and her faith in God drove people to like her more. During her time at the sewing factory, she became convinced to go back to school. And so she did but with only her own support. She financed her GED and finished that path on her own. She knew that she had an avenue to make it to college, a rare occurrence in that small town. But money again was an issue. She persevered, by working and gaining as many scholarships as possible. Her spirit pushed her to keep moving forward. She pursued a degree in accounting, with the goal of becoming Mexico's equivalent of a CPA. My father was able to attain this. Although it was a struggle for him, it seemed unsurmountable to my mother. She took the challenge head on. She was one of nine people in the course. Attending college in Mexico was rare in those days outside of the few of higher socioeconomic class who already had the means to fund their children's college education.

My mom's family did not have the means to help fund her endeavors, not even a ride to school, so she had to carpool to school every day with one of the neighbors. This did not help her in her status in class, and people were open to express their "superiority" to her, all because they came from money and she didn't. My mom tried to prove to them that it didn't matter to her, but it did. She had to deal with the weight of that daily, and she would constantly hear her neighbor bad-mouth her to the other classmates.

Those comments did not affect her as much as the lack of resources to pay for classes did. She couldn't make up the money for her last few semesters and knew she had to drop out. She had no way of making the payments on time, and so she broke down at the dean's office. She didn't break down as a cry for help, rather of disappointment at telling the dean she had to withdraw from the course. The dean opened his door and heard the news that one of the course's best students was going to drop out. He refused to accept that as the end of her journey, so he worked on a plan to grant her more scholarship funding, and he did. At the point where my mom had no more hope left to finish, a gracious person stepped in and filled her with more. She believed it to be God's intervention and became forever grateful to her dean for being a good man of God. And every time I go home, I ask to see her binder where she did all of her assignments, just as a reminder of that moment in her life, as it is something I wish to relay to my future kids about how perseverant their grandmother was.

Her faith is unwavering, not just in herself but in God. She still recounts stories of how her faith has been carved by this youth ministry she served in during her teen years. While in this group she met a man, a priest, who had a good impact on her soul. Padre Fili was his name. I had the pleasure of meeting him during one of our family trips and could tell from his presence alone that he is a good-natured soul with purity in his heart. He's a short stocky man with a round belly and a round face. His cheeks are full and sit high on his face to not allow his eyes to fully open. His overall shape is reminiscent to those of the fat happy Buddha statues. Funny, considering he is a Catholic priest. He was balding when I met him, and I can't picture him with hair at any point in his life. It wouldn't suit him anyways. He had a distinct deep voice that mended wisdom, authority, and sincerity in every word he said. His smile was genuine and filled with joy that showed his love for life and for his faith. I'm sure he sits well in God's court, and he has a place set for him in Heaven. She would recount how she would be crying and share some of her traumas with Padre Fili and the youth group, and Padre Fili would have the ability to calm her mind. He made such a strong impact on her that she asked him to be the priest to wed her to my father.

Nobody else in her family was as devout a Catholic as her. She would constantly go to church by herself or with maybe a few siblings but rarely would the whole family go as a complete unit. My father's household was different. It was in a sense required for them to go. My dad found faith by heritage and loyalty to his parents; my mom found faith by the yearning in her soul. There was much in my mom's life to mourn, but like my father, she never quit in her journey. I admire her as much, if not more, than my dad. She has a passion in her soul that cannot be quelled. She lives life with an intensity that is difficult to describe without meeting her but also balances that with such compassion in her heart. If somebody is asking for help, her first instinct is to find out how she can help. These words don't do her justice as her spirit cannot be measured or fully explained by words. She has taught me to live life with vigor, with passion and with faith. She dealt with much turmoil in her heart throughout her life and can understand of the struggles of the soul.

My story up to this point does not compare to either of my parents. I have been blessed with the opportunities this country has given me and with having the two best role models by my side through it all. I feel ashamed for feeling stuck in this pit of depression and anxiety as they can only witness me from the sidelines. There is nothing they can do to help pick me up from this. They deserve to see me happy, but better they deserve to know that I am happy and happy for myself, not for them. I wish to give them the gift of knowing that. Seeing what I inherited from them makes me realize the potential I have in this world. And no matter how many times I hear them say they are proud of me. I can only accept it after I can be proud of myself.

My dad and I decide to grab some food before finishing the drive to the hotel. I ask where he wants to go eat and he chooses In-n-Out. The line is always long, but he doesn't care. He probably picked that spot on purpose to be able to spend the most time with me as possible. And I am happy to oblige, and I pay for his meal. I wanted to give him more, but he was content with that alone.

"Thanks for giving me a ride, Dad. I know you didn't have to."

"I don't mind. I'll take this ride every weekend with you."

"Thanks, Dad. I love you."

"I love you too, son."

The pictures of me when I was a baby pop up in my head with him holding me in his arms. I can just see his smile in every photo and that look is what I see in him across the dinner table now. I'll remember this for the rest of my life, I'll remember this. He recounts more stories of him and his childhood, and I listen and soak up as much as I can. As I see him across the table, I notice something; he's aging.

Everybody's time in this world is finite and I can see Father Time catching up to him and my mother. They have weathered many storms and it shows. I feel a bit sad because of this inevitability. I've known this for a long time, but seeing him and his head full of grey hair and more distinguished wrinkles in his face makes the fact much more apparent. My time with them in this world is starting to run slim. I think of how often I see them and how many chances I'll have to spend more moments like this with them. I hate to think there's a finite number. I start to plead with God in my head to grant me more time with them. I want time to stop right now, so I can enjoy this moment without it affecting their finite time. It's hard to even think about, but I know it's something I must accept, and it's partially the reason why I asked my dad to tell me about his life. I want to be able to paint the picture of him and my mom of how I see them. But as I think about their time in this world coming to an end, I find some hope in that bit of despair. They are also aware of the time they have left in this world, and they choose to fill it with as much time as possible with their children. Knowing that this time is finite makes them more precious. And I can't taint that by asking God for more time with them. Rather I should choose to enjoy the present and the waning moments I have left with them. So I snap out of it, and just enjoy my dad's company.

We finish dinner and head to the hotel as we are ready to wind it down for the night. We get checked in and finally have a chance to get settled in, but I find it difficult to sleep.

Through the highs and lows of the day I find myself wanting to reconcile a bit more with my dad. So I say, "Dad, I just want to say sorry."

"For what, mi hjio?"

"For making it hard for you guys. I know I don't seem the happiest right now, and I don't want to make you guys worried."

"It's ok, mi hijo. Life brings us down every once and a while, but we'll be here for you."

"Thanks, Dad."

It gives me enough peace to be able to shut my eyes for the night.

Retreat

THE MORNING COMES, AND THE day starts off with a calm feeling. I get to sleep in, and the break from the normal schedule refreshes my mind. My body has gotten accustomed to waking up in the darkness and still am able to beat the sunrise even with the extra hour or two of sleep. I made it this far, and for that I am relieved. My dad wakes up a few moments later, and we both get ready to leave for the airport. A few more hours and I'll be thousands of miles away, away from the dulling pressure of this place, away from the skewed perspectives, away from my normal life. I start thinking of things to do in Hawaii, like where I should eat and places I should see, but I don't want a traditional tourist experience. I'm going there to find my own path and answer my own questions, not to follow the crowd. What do I want to bring back from Hawaii? The answer is simple for me, direction. I need the plan laid out for me, or rather I need to lay that plan out for myself. No more complacency when it comes to the direction of my life. I must remain open-minded to whatever this retreat will show me, to what God will show me. Who will I become, or rather who have I become? Who do I want to be?

We get to the airport, and my dad gives me his farewells.

"All right, son, have fun. Enjoy the time off, ok?"

"Thanks, Dad. I will. I'll take pictures and make sure to enjoy my time there."

"Good. We love you. Call when you get there, ok?"

"Ok."

I make it to security and have to wait an hour or so to board. An hour to myself, I never knew how beautiful free time is, time not connected to any pressure of figuring out action items, or chores, or keeping up with work, or any other restraining thought. Immediately, I feel less pressure on my shoulders and can see a bit more clearly. Was this all I needed? Just a little break? I've put forth much effort these last few years but into what exactly? Nothing of substance, just material success and status. I felt like I had nothing else to strive for, no goals in sight and no purpose to hold myself back. So the need to continue to progress, the need to move regardless of direction, that's what forced me into this pit. I don't know how to quell it, that fire in my soul to move to never stop. I've dug myself into this pit for that reason alone. But for this short time, I can grab on to a bit more hope. For when I learn to control the tenacity of my spirit and finally learn to channel it, then I will be able to reach the heights of my potential. That soul will not stop until the heart in my chest stops beating, and even then, it might give a bit more. I've seen it all this time as a curse, but I will learn to change it into a blessing. I can't help but think that my soul has rebelled against me and the chaos I have given it. I wish to understand its quarrels fully and intend to correct it, to grant it peace, for it deserves it for merely pulling me up from those deep waters time and time again.

The plane is ready for boarding, and I get my seat. The seat is small, but I'm next to the window so at least I'll have a view for the flight. I have one flight to LAX and another to Honolulu with another big layover in between. As I sit waiting for the plane to move, I put my headphones on and listen to some music. Music has always been there for me, as a little escape to my own world. It has been the vessel in which I pour the emotions I cannot express to the world or when nobody has been there to listen, or rather when I wanted nobody to listen. A few minutes go by, and I settle down into my chair, continuing to look outside the window. More minutes go and I feel nothing and still see the same still image of the airport in the plane.

As people are waiting, some with a bit less patience than others, I feel something a bit different. I feel a calming sensation, one reminiscent to the morning. No anticipation for the plane to move. Hell, I'd feel the same if I stared out that same view for hours. No anxiety for how high we will climb into the air. I feel present, clear, in the moment. The past and future do not exist as I have suspended any thoughts or memories. I recognize this, and a slight smile appears on my face. The plane stays idle for a few moments longer, enough for me to absorb this feeling completely, and then finally I feel the brakes disengage. That still image has gone as the plane begins moving towards the runway. The tires on the plane react to every inconsistency on the concrete underneath our feet, and it grows the anticipation of every person in the plane. I give into that feeling as well. The plane picks up speed gradually, making those bumps on the road feel a bit sharper as we all get tossed around slightly the faster we go. The wings move their flaps into position, and the moment I feel the plane can't go any faster, it surprises me as I feel another jolt of acceleration.

The wind breaking across the surface of the plane and the spin of the turbines are all I can hear as they drown out all the other ambient noise from inside the plane. The runway must be miles long it seems as the plane continues to gain speed, and then finally I feel my seat tip back slightly and with it a pressure that pushes me farther into my seat. The plane has taken off. As it makes its way to cruising altitude, I see the view of the airport shifts more and more the higher we ascend. The sight outside the window is beautiful, for it shows the city in such a different view. All the structures from the main city that seem so tall at ground level, slowly lose their height advantage over us. The plane ascends gradually, and the city gets covered with clouds as we even climb past them. The clouds seem so soft from where we are as they create such a unique texture, one that entices you to reach out and grab it to feel it. And as we ascend, the weight of anything holding me down to this world has gone with it, losing its reach on me, even for the moment. I feel at peace.

The flight does not last long, maybe an hour and half, but I find it enjoyable. I resign myself to enjoy the moment in the air. I can feel the downward tip of the plane indicating its descent. The clouds covered the view throughout the flight, and so as we descend past them it feels like the veil over the city of L.A. has been uncovered. The size of the city itself is something to marvel at. I wish there was enough time this trip to stop here and explore all this city has to offer, but I must save that for another time, for this is not my final destination. The descent takes us fifteen minutes and is peaceful. I feel my mind and body refreshed already just from the new stimulus of the plane and the view of the city. I feel the initial impact of the landing gear hit the strip and I feel happy for making it to the first milestone of the trip. I realize as I land that I will have a lot of time to myself while I wait around for the next flight. The layover is at the sweet spot of not having enough time to leave the airport and exploring what is around and having too much time to want to wait at the airport. I grab my bag and don't feel any rush to get out of the plane, as I know I will be itching to find things to do. I get out of the plane and start researching what things there are to do in Hawaii. I see a host of tourist attractions, and I am hesitant to try those things. But then I remember something. I remember a judo sensei I had once trained with back in Reno, named Akamu.

Immediately I remember of the fond memories I had the pleasure of having with him. They were memories of an old life in which I had less weight on my shoulders and I put fewer restrictions on myself. Akamu is a gentle character, one to always smile no matter how hard life becomes. He is a stockier man, around five feet nine inches, around the same height as me. He looks to be around two hundred to two hundred and twenty pounds at any given time but can move like lightning. Our sparring matches weren't really matches, more like a cat toying with its food before deciding to kill it, and I was the food. He would always be gentle outside of the mat, and even in it he was well respected by everybody.

The moments in the mats were ones to remember, but the moments with him outside of the mats were ones I'll never forget. When they lived in town, his wife became a certified hot Pilates instructor and he recruited some people from the dojo to go and support. Of course, I was one. I didn't know what I was signing up for, but upon entering I remember getting into a sauna with the heat set at 100–110 degrees Fahrenheit with a slew of beautiful women all ready to take the class. Initially, I thought it to be a win, but shortly after the class started, I was humbled very quickly. Within ten minutes of the class, I just wanted to get out of the room and could not distinguish between my own sweat and tears. It was a challenge like no other and those who commit to that form of exercise have eternally gained my respect.

I wished I had more adventures like that with him while he was here, but the time was cut short as he relocated to the northwest. One thing that will always stick with me is a phrase he would occasionally say, "If can, can. If no can, no can. And if no can, still can." To this day, I have yet to understand the full meaning of it, but I try to apply it to similar situations in which he used it.

As I sit in the airport waiting for the time to speed up, I message him, hoping to hear from him soon. Not too long after he responds.

"Hey, sensei. How are you?"

I still call him sensei over his name. I feel it natural to do so.

"I'm good. How are things with you?"

"Good, good. Actually, heading to your home island, Oahu."

"Really? You should have let us know. We were planning a trip down there soon."

"Oh, well, next time I head back, I'll be sure to get with you first. Hey, sensei, what should I do while I'm down there?"

"Well, there are a lot of things like these awesome hiking trails by the central part of the island. My favorite is Manoa Falls. It's an easy hike, but it's really pretty once you get to the end of it. If you want a challenge try Koko Head." He proceeds to tell me about a dozen more hikes and I get more and more excited as he does.

"I'll have to see if I can get all of those in while I'm down there. What about food? Anything I have to try before leaving?"

"Ooohh, I know you love sweets so you have to find the original Leonard's Bakery. Actually, I just remembered, I have a good friend from college down there who has time between jobs. He's a cool guy, and I think you guys would get along well. He's an engineer, too. I'll see if I can get you two to link up while you're down there."

"Honestly, that would be amazing. I appreciate if you could set that up for me."

"All right. I'll keep you posted."

I become excited to hear the response, but he doesn't respond for a while. He still gives me many options to see the island as it was intended so for that I am more than grateful. I look at the clock and it only moved an hour. I still have plenty of time left to burn. It gives me a few moments to reflect on judo and all that it has done for me.

A sport as popular around the world as soccer, one that trains not just my body but my mind. It has taught me true humility in many ways. How did I get started and what made me stick with it? Back then, when I was fresh out of college, I realized of how bland I was, for I had less fog covering my eyes and less noise drowning out the voice of my heart and soul. I knew of my naivety, of not knowing much about life, but I did not understand how low I stood in the rankings of knowledge. My soul always wants to explore positions of discomfort and vulnerability. At times, I have become damaged because of it. But this time, it was to repair what I lost, my confidence. I was invited to judo by an old coworker. He was aware that I was not in the best emotional state and he offered to take me. I didn't have an excuse to say no so I agreed.

The first day I went, I remember of how different the environment had felt. I was nervous—of course I was—but everybody there reassured me. Everybody had a humility to them as they all understood my position of being the new guy. Everything was new to me, from the clothes to even the simple movements. I didn't even know how to tumble or break fall correctly. I was sore and tired as my body was not used to moving the way judo requires, but even so, I felt like a kid again. Every forward tumble and backward roll brought me back to my childhood when I would roll down the grassy hills in the parks by the schools. Every throw I took reminded me of when I would jump out of the swings at the right time to see how high I could reach. I fell in love with it, I did. It provided my mind and my body with a new stimulus and it gave my soul something to progress in. Most importantly, it helped relieve the pains in my heart, as if to say that the pains my body takes will help hide the damage I feel internally.

As I grew into this sport, I felt my being evolve, as I learned more and more about this sport and I started to understand that the humility that my sensei and other judoka have demonstrated to me. Time continued to move forward, and my heart has had its scars closed, and I finally had felt a bit of relief from those woes. I felt complete, like I have climbed higher in the ladder of knowledge and my soul had enough to keep its urges satisfied. However, my mistake—my grave mistake—has been that I believed this to be singular, a one-time process. Complacency is what drove me to these depths. And now I leave for an unknown place in an effort to clear that reminiscent fog that has covered my eyes. There are only about thirty more minutes before embarking, and so I just sit and reflect on this. I know how I got here. One answer has been revealed to me already, and for that I am grateful. Now the journey begins, to climb back up and to build myself into a being that can withstand the tides of that ocean.

The plane finally gets called to board and excitement fills me. I get up and begin to jitter. I get my bag and head to the plane. As I take my seat, I am able to see across the window, night time has covered the city and the city lights fill the view. They imitate the stars in the sky but with less glory and less purity, but even so they are still beautiful to see. I get an aisle seat, but I ask the person next to me for the window seat and they are happy to oblige. The same sensations of the first flight come back to me as we prepare to fly. We begin the lift off, and the city lights show just how big LA is. The lights make everything seem intertwined with each other. It shows just how vast the city really is, and I bid it farewell for the moment. In a few hours, I'll be in Hawaii and hoping that God will praise me with even more answers.

The flight lasts all night it seems, and the excitement subsides slightly. I find my body more tired than usual, so I close my eyes and rest for a bit, hoping that when I wake, we will be in Hawaii. Time goes by until I finally open my eyes. I'm still in the air, but I see new lights beneath us. They are scarcer than in LA, but they provide a picture of the silhouette of the islands. They are much more subtle to the eyes and more inviting to see. I can't see much else of the islands as the darkness of the night drapes over them. I wish to see the true beauty of the island soon. Not much time passes until we hit the landing strip. Finally, I am here.

With my first step onto the island, I feel the warm breeze, I smell the ocean mist in the air, and the humidity is nice enough to stay out all night if I wasn't tired. I'm relieved to have gotten here. As my phone gets a signal again, I see that my sensei reached out to me.

"Hey, so I talked to my friend, and he's free this week. Here's his info so you guys can figure out what you want to do."

"Thanks, sensei. I appreciate all that you've done for me." I meant it, but not just for reaching out to his friend, for everything he has done for me.

I make it to the hotel, and instantly I tell myself, "While I'm this far from home, I don't want to spend too much time here. The answers I search are not in a bland room." I unwind for the night as I just look out the window trying to distinguish anything in the dark of night, but there isn't much but the moonlight and the silhouette of the mountains. Even that is more beautiful than I could have imagined. Serenity, the only word I could use to describe it. Tomorrow, I will embark on exploring this place. I lay my head to rest and already feel peace oozing into my soul.

The morning rises, and I get up with a giddy joy, ready to explore. It's Sunday and after talking to my sensei's friend, we are not set to meet until Monday morning, so today I am on my own. I realize I forgot to call my parents when I landed so I decide to give them a quick call. (*Ring. Ring. Ring.* No answer.)

"Hey, Mom and Dad, just wanted to call and let you know I made it to Hawaii. I haven't had much of a chance to check it out, I got in late last night. But I'll be sure to take a bunch of pictures and send them to you guys. I know you're probably busy so just call when you can. I love you."

I get my backpack ready and take a look at the list my sensei gave me. Manoa Falls, that's what I will see first. Before I go, I need to find a few supplies, so I head to the corner store right across the street, and for the first time, I get to feel the presence of Hawaii. There is such a serene ambiance everywhere, and things grow out of every crevice from the ground. I'm not even by the main area of vegetation, but there is so much life here that it grows where it can. It's a perfect seventy degrees, and there is a slight breeze that brings the freshness of the ocean with it. I get what I need at the store and call for an Uber to get me to the trailhead. The Uber driver is a tan middle-aged man. He seems like an average build, maybe a bit slimmer, and speaks very gently but also invites conversation. He personified the type of person I would think I would meet in the island.

We drive away from the tourist area that the hotel is located in and the farther we go the more I see the true culture of this place. The people walking along are all calm, tethered to the roots of the ground, as if to say they are also part of the island's roots. We drive down older streets and see the older houses, the ones that have been there for ages.

I ask my Uber driver, "These houses look a bit older. How long have they been around?"

"Oh, these houses have been here for a long time. Probably right around the 1930s or 40s."

"Wow, they all kind of look similar, but are all different once you keep your eyes on them for a while."

"Hawaiian culture has a lot of Asian roots, a lot of Japanese influence. That's why they all kind of look the same."

"Yeah, they're all bunched together, too. There's no room for yards even."

"Yeah, the properties here are prime real estate. It's in the center of Oahu and close to everything. Plus, the nostalgia I guess adds to the price."

"Really? How much does one of these houses go for?"

"Oh, you're looking at close to one million dollars for some of these small lots."

"Jeez, that's crazy. How do people afford to live here?"

"Well, there's a few areas away from the center that are a bit cheaper, but it's not easy to get a house here, at least not anymore."

"What do people do for work around here, like besides tourism and whatnot? I would assume there's a lot of jobs around the ports and fishing."

"Yeah, that and there are a lot more jobs in construction. There are a lot more buildings and roads that are being built. Trying to fit more people here. Plus, all the old roads are beginning to uproot from all the plants and trees growing."

"Yeah, that makes a lot of sense. Has this place grown a lot since you've been here?"

"Yeah, a lot. A lot more people from the mainland here."

"Who wouldn't want to live here? I'd move here, too if it wasn't for the crazy house prices."

"Yeah, the locals here aren't very happy with all that's growing here. We're a small island after all, and we like it that way."

"I see, so you guys don't like too many tourists, then, do you?"

"I don't mind, that's how I've made my money with this Uber gig. But some people just don't like how things change."

"Well, I appreciate all that you've told me until now. I hope that I'm not asking too many questions."

"Oh no, you seem like a nice kid. Very good spirit in you."

Those few words fill my spirit a little bit.

"What brings you to Hawaii, by the way?"

"Well, I came because I wanted to get away from the chaos at home. And I wanted to find something here."

"Oh, and what is that something."

"Peace."

"This place can help, but peace is something we find on the inside. I'm sure you'll find it soon enough."

"We'll see."

The closer we get to the mountain ridge, the vegetation ramps up and makes it seem like the houses are being slowly swallowed by the island. There's not enough land for all that wants to grow as life bursts in every direction. The terrain rejects civilization as the pipes have become uprooted, pushed away from the growing vegetation underneath it. Now that I can see them clearly, the mountains explode up from the ground with no gradual incline. They shoot out from the ground to try and touch the heavens, and it seems like heaven could actually be on the tops of some of these mountains for how high they reach. I can imagine the trails will be more difficult because of this. As we get to the base of the ridge, human intervention becomes more and more scarce. Eventually, the only signs of human life are the trails blazed by the ones before me. He drops me off, and we wish each other a farewell.

Manoa Falls, I'm only about a mile away from seeing the end of the trailhead. From what the Uber driver and my sensei have told me, it's a sight to see. So I begin to walk. The vegetation is so unique to me, especially coming from a place with very little greenery. The trees and shrubs all come in various sizes and shapes. The rain from the last few weeks has made the soil very soft. Every inch of the mountain is covered with layers upon layers of green. To the right of me is a small stream that accompanies me through the entire trailhead. I try to walk fast at first because of the excitement of trying to see the end of the trail but slow down to try and take in all that I see as I know I may not ever see this again. These two mentalities take turns until I finally reach the end of the trail. What a sight it is. I know what I laid my eyes on cannot be fully described by mere words, but I will try to do it justice.

Manoa Falls is a steep waterfall. It looks like it starts from the middle of the sky as I can't see the top from the base of the waterfall. The stream is slim and runs down this vertical wall. The wall has a distinct bricked texture. Its edges have been worn down from the small stream. Every time the stream hits these small ridges in the wall it creates a mist that covers the main streamline and plays with the sunlight to make it look like a veil of light. As the stream finishes its descent from the heavens, it fills a small pool. When it hits that pool, it creates a serene melody that my ears immediately hone in on. It tunes out every other noise. My heartbeat slows as it matches the natural rhythm of the stream. I feel as if this place is a glimpse of what heaven would feel like. No regrets, no remorse, no thoughts, just a feeling of bliss. My heart, my mind, my body, and my soul, they are all in sync. I could sit here all day and just listen to the stream hit the pond at the bottom. I stay and just soak it all in. I stay for about ten minutes, just feeling the presence of this place, and it feels like hours. The only reason I leave is because I realize that there is much more to see on the island and more places that have this bliss.

I head down the trailhead, and then I see a small path a bit hidden from all the trees and vines. It doesn't have a trail sign, or maybe it was just hidden underneath the vines and leaves, so I am a bit hesitant to go. But I'm intrigued, and I did not come all this way to play things safe. It would be an insult if I left anything in doubt here. So with that in mind, I head to that path, ducking over and under the initial vines and trees that cover the entrance to the trail. The trail is a bit narrow and engulfed in all the bamboo and roots from the trees allowing the trail to be filled with shade, which is nice seeing it is the hottest part of the day. The topsoil is saturated and makes my shoes sink a few inches with every step. The roots and vines on the ground are covered with a touch of this soil and decrease the traction of my shoes. The trail steadily climbs the mountain wall, so it makes me diligent in every step I take so as to not slip and fall into the forest of bamboo. To distract myself from the slight fear of falling, I want to listen to my music. I put my earphones in, and I instantly feel disconnected to it as my ears reject the noise. My soul wants to stay connected to this place and thinks that any distraction from this is insulting. I put my earbuds back in my bag, and then I stop for a moment. I close my eyes and just listen. Then the wind excites the terrain. The percussion begins with the leaves rustling. Then my ears hone in on the collisions between bamboo trees, creating a bass for the orchestra. Birds hidden within the trees provide the vocals. This is what music tries to emulate, the sound of nature. It excites my spirit as I finally am able to hear it call out to me, "You are home." My legs move again.

I have been trekking for about three hours, and I finally see the end of the trail as the trees break and open up the sky once again. I see the last small hill I need to climb to get to the end of the trail. I make it up there and make it to the top of the

mountain. The forest breaks and allows me to see the terrain…
how beautiful. The entire place is eerily reminiscent like I've
been here before, or rather I've felt this before. With it brings
the soothing ocean scent, one to unlock many old memories and
tie them to this place. The wind is soothing, as the first breeze
caresses my skin. My body feels light, as if I could go with the
wind if I so choose, but the roots I trail over take a hold on me,
creating such a serene dichotomy in my heart. It's as if no matter
where I choose to go, to unite with the wind or to spread the
roots of my feet through the soil, I would be happy, to. I am
happy here. The sun illuminates the skyline and light radiates
from the clouds. The clouds dance around the tall mountain
that sets across my sight as I still can't see the top of it, even at
this elevation. I think, *Not a single thing made by human hands
can hold a candle to this, for this has been forged by God's hands.* It
truly does feel like home.

I have to head back before it gets too dark. The trail back is
just as beautiful as the way up. I see my old path and instantly
remind myself of where I almost fell or where the mud filled
my shoes or when I heard the choir of nature at its clearest. It
takes me another hour or so to trek back to civilization. As I
finally make it back to the base of the trail and wait for another
Uber, I look back at everything I have experienced in such a
short time here. It begins to rain, not heavy, just a light mist but
still enough to form a small puddle in front of my feet. The rain
is warm on my skin and feel refreshing after a long day of trail
hiking. As I look down at the dark reflection of myself, I notice
something that I haven't seen a long time, a smile. My shoes are
full of dirt and mud and I'm full of sweat, but that smile on my
face is real. What a blessing this trip has treated me to, and it's

only day one. The Uber gets here, and I finally head back to the hotel and want to keep exploring the city, but tomorrow will have much more in store for me, I'm sure.

Another night of good rest refreshes my body from the heavy day yesterday as I am up and ready to move. I get my phone and make sure the plans I made with my sensei's friend are still in the works. He responds with a yes and is on the way to the hotel. Immediately, I wonder what he has in store, a person from the island who knows much about this place. I pack my bag and head downstairs to wait for him to show. He finally arrives in a small white sedan. I immediately knew it was him as he was the only one on the street and the only car parked in front of the hotel lobby. He invites me in the car, and we introduce ourselves,

"Hey man, I'm…"

"Hey what's up? I'm Kekoa."

Kekoa is a darker-skinned man of Filipino descent, but I would not have known if he did not tell me. He is a bit shorter than I am, standing close to five feet five inches, and has a slim build and sports a thin mustache. Kekoa and I start talking about how we met our mutual acquaintance. I know him as sensei, but Kekoa knows him as Akamu. I always thought it was a nickname for so long, but turns out it wasn't. Kekoa has known him much longer than I have and can speak about him much more than I can.

"So how did you meet Akamu?"

"Oh, we had some of the same classes in college. We both got degrees at the University of Hawaii here. He tells me you're an engineer, too."

"Yeah, I studied back in Reno. Been doing it for some time now."

"Oh nice. Akamu told me you guys met through judo. That must be a fun time."

"Yeah, he's a great instructor, until you have to spar against him. Then it's just trying to survive Haha."

"Haha, yeah, he's always been really good and competitive with it. I used to train with him for a little bit."

"Oh really? I didn't know. How high up the ranks did you get?"

"Oh, I wasn't anything special. I only got to about a blue belt. But it's really fun with the right group of people."

"Yeah, I agree. Luckily, I have an awesome dojo I train at back home. Have you ever been to the mainland?"

"Only once, actually to help Akamu move out of Reno."

"Oh really? That's ironic. How did you like it?"

"It nice, definitely different, but I enjoyed it. I'd like to plan another trip up to visit him, maybe get all three of us together."

"Yeah, man, we'd be the three musketeers. That would be epic."

He has been consistent to himself. How Kekoa sees Akamu is the same way I do. As we talk, we find more and more things in common with each other, as we segue conversation away from Akamu and to the present. Kekoa has a friendly presence that makes it very easy to engage him in conversation. As we start talking, we grow a bit of kinship and mutual respect for each other.

The farther we drive, the farther we get from civilization and the horizon fills with only blue skies and blue seas. I roll the windows down to feel the ocean breeze on my skin, and it's more refreshing than ice cold water on a summer day. The road parallels the shoreline and before we make it to our final destination, we stop midway to a place called Lanai Lookout. It is a more mainstream lookout but is still beyond anything I have seen. The sandy beaches end abruptly and are replaced by stones that are smooth and overlay on top of each other as if to mimic the ocean waves but frozen in time. The waves don't seem to crash in, rather they slide and gradually ride the small incline of the land. I sit here on one of the small ledges and just breathe. I feel as if the more I explore, the more I can just stay and admire the beauty of a singular place.

Before we decide to leave, I ask Kekoa, "How can you live here and not be out here all the time? This place is freaking beautiful, man. Even the small bushes seem pretty to me."

He responds, "We are used to seeing these things all the time, but sometimes when fresh eyes come to see it for the first time, we can feed off of it and experience a bit of that as well."

It made me think of showing a kid a cool trick and seeing the excitement in their eyes, and it infects us and makes us excited as well. Happiness and vigor are infectious I come to realize. We stay for about fifteen minutes than continue on to get to the main part of the journey for the day.

More driving turns those sandy beaches and smooth shorelines into mountain ridges that interact with the tides much more. The luscious green that surrounds the central part of the island is not as present here, if it weren't for the ocean to the side of us, I would consider this part of Nevada. The mountains are more bare and some of the trees don't have as many leaves. The shrubs are reminiscent of sagebrush, looking a bit more exotic but still have a sense of requiring fewer nutrients to survive. I would not think that a place that is surrounded by the ocean would have a terrain like this. It offers a bit more of a homey feeling as this is familiar to the Sierra Mountains. Kekoa parks the car on a side of the road and points to me the top of the hike, Makapu'u Lighthouse. It sits on top of the island's easternmost point and

oversees the ocean. The hike is steep, on paved road at least with
no shade at all but is short enough for me to almost run up it.
I look at Kekoa as if I'm about to hop on to a carnival ride, and
I begin the trail. I have to curtail my excitement so Kekoa can
keep up or else I would have already been at the top.

We talk a bit more about life. The topics we discuss aren't
important as I can't recall a single thing. We pass the time, and
we make it to the top of the mountain. It was a lot shorter than
what I expected, which was a bit of a pleasant surprise. I get
to the top of the lookout and am able to see half of the island
looking one way and the vast ocean the other. The opposing
views play well with each other, that although civilization is
only a few miles away from the vast ocean, it doesn't matter.
They know their place in this world, and it is one to just sit back
and admire the views that God has granted them. It gets a bit
crowded, and I decide to leave as it ruins the scenery a bit for
me. So right away from the paved roads are some unique rock
ledges that for some reason I want to climb onto. I get halfway
and sit down with my feet over the safer part of the ledge and
just watch the tides hit the base of the mountain. The waves play
a small melody whose rhythm has been engraved on my mind
through my ears. The silky ocean surface turns to a cloudy white
as it hits the mountain wall. And as I look down, something tells
me to get to the farthest part of the ledge. I oblige as I get up and
move closer to the farthest point. I need to maneuver a bit and
take a few risky steps. I don't want to look down until I make it
to stable ground. I finally make it, as if this was longer than the
trail I just hiked yesterday. I sit down. Then from the corner of
my eye, I am able to see the lighthouse. The views distracted me
from realizing there was actually one here this whole time. The

lighthouse sits about fifty feet below the mountain's top point but sits alone on the easternmost point of the island.

Immediately, my mind thinks this is the final destination. *Have I finally reached that place? Am I really that close?* There is only one way to find out. It doesn't seem like a far hike from here, but there doesn't seem to be any access points to it. So I ask Kekoa who this whole time was taking pictures of the view and of me on this ledge.

"Hey, is there any way to get to that lighthouse down there?"

"There should be. I think there is a smaller trail that branches off from this one a bit lower down."

So we walk back down the steep hill, and I see what he is talking about. There is a small trail that seems to be lurking behind this small and worn pillbox. I immediately point it out to Kekoa, and we begin the second part of the trail.

As we journey along, we reach a fence. "No trespassing allowed." My initial thought is to just turn around, but I did not travel thousands of miles to be stopped by a measly fence and a single sign.

So I tell Kekoa, "I'm going to climb over."

"Really? Are you sure about that?"

"Yeah, I'm sure. It even looks like there are some steps here by the wall that you can use to get over without touching the barbed wires. People have tried before me, so I might as well give it a go."

"All right. Well, let's do this then. Doesn't seem like there much sense in talking you out of it."

"You're coming with? You don't have to."

"No, man, I want to see how crazy you are. Plus, you need somebody just in case you get in trouble."

"Don't have to tell me twice, but thank you."

So we head over this fence, and the vertical wall to the side of us looks like there could be chunks of rocks that could break off at any time, which would make sense as to why it was fenced off. But I did not hesitate. I am this close to the lighthouse, and I need to find out if this is it. We get within thirty feet of this lighthouse and stumble across another fence. It extends past the ledge and has barbed wires on both top and bottom. At first glance, there is no way to get in there, but again, I am not quitting.

Kekoa even notes, "Maybe we shouldn't go there. It doesn't seem like there is a place to get past this fence."

"Trust me. I'll find a way to get past this."

I am so sure of it that I said it with full confidence. I analyze the ledge where the fence extends past it, and I notice there are some areas that can be used as footholds. I also see breaks in the barbed wire where I can place my hands. I immediately sit down and climb on the ledge and take hold of the fence bar. I take a few more steps down so that I can dip my head underneath the fence bar and start to pull myself back up to the ground. I finally made it here.

I see the lighthouse, and I just stare at it. I analyze every brick it was formed from. It overlooks the ocean, almost out of pride in knowing that its waters can never fully reach it. The white paint is chipping off at certain points but still looks fresh. The windows at the top of it have a small foggy tint, maybe because of the ocean breeze and permanent water stains. I stand in front of it, asking it, "Is this where I need to be? Is this the end of my journey?" I calm myself down and try to open my ears to the natural sounds of the oceans and the winds. I try to crack open my heart to allow it to be filled with any emotion, and I try to reduce my ego so that my soul can breathe here. "*Your journey has not yet finished. You have many more steps to take and many more mountains to climb. This is not the end, nor is this your final destination.*" That voice. It is the same one that had awoken me from the depths of despair. Is this…God?

"God, is that you? Are you the one speaking to me?" I stay looking up at the sky for a moment, hoping for a response. I hear nothing in return, but I stay here a few moments longer and just let those words seep into my soul. Once I feel refreshed, not just physically, but emotionally and spiritually, I head back with Kekoa.

"Man, I can't believe you did that. You're a wild man."

"No, I just saw something that I had to do, and I did it."

He doesn't understand the extent of that statement, but we traverse back.

Before we go all the way back to the car, Kekoa points out a unique formation of rocks at the base of the mountain, the tide pools. It is at the bottom of an almost vertical descent down the side of the mountain, but we both decide to do it. There is a slight trail that has been carved by the countless of footsteps that have had the same idea as me and Kekoa, so it aids us in getting there. We have to watch our feet as the trail is filled with a lot of loose gravel, but we see some people in front of us and note how they are getting down and follow a similar path. The trail down is fun, as if trying to figure out the maze to the secret treasure. We get down, and, luckily, I have brought an extra set of clothes, so I have no hesitation to jump into the water. The pools are small and shallow but still deep enough to float without touching the bottom. They are enclosed by rings of old mountain walls that have sunk past the ocean floor. The water is salty, even more so as there is less access for the water to flow freely. But it is still refreshing. The first time I get in the water in Hawaii, and it could not have come at any better time. The best moment is floating in the water, with a few small fish all around us, and the tide hits the edge of the wall and sprays a blissful mist over the pool. Each droplet that touches my skin relieves more and more pressure from my shoulders. With each wave of mists, my body loses pent up tension, as if healing old injuries and aches. I glance at Kekoa. He wears a smile on his face, as if he is experiencing this for the first time as well. I don't know how long we spend there as time feels dilated, but Kekoa keeps an eye on the clock, and his belly tells him that he is hungry.

"What do you feel like eating?"

"Honestly, I'm game for whatever. As long as it is good, I'm not too picky."

"Ok. Poke it is."

We get out of the pools as he tells me to watch out for the small urchins that hide in the crevices of the walls. I dry up and get dressed as we have to make the vertical climb back up. I didn't feel too tired out, but in the middle of the day and already traversing the mountains for a few hours, I feel the exertion on my body. It didn't help that the pool relaxed my muscles, so they aren't as ready to fire and move up this wall, but we make it up nonetheless. We start to drive back into town, and he stops at a random shopping center parking lot. There doesn't seem to be any restaurants here, and the main attraction is a Walgreens.

"Is this where we're going to eat?" I ask.

"We're going to pick up some snacks here."

As he says this, I spot a pink food truck at the corner of the lot. The paint is a bit dulled, but it still contrasts anything else around. The logo letters read "Leonard's Bakery" on the side painted in teal. The truck has some miles on it as some of the rivets that hold the walls are starting to rust with a few missing even. The wheel hubs are all rusted out as well.

"Hey, Akamu told me about this. Portuguese donuts, right?"

"Yeah, they're the best place in town for some quick sweets. They come super fresh, too. They make them to order."

My mouth begins to water thinking about it.

"Yeah, I could go for some food, and I'm always in the mood for dessert."

"You'll like this, then."

My excitement grows from nothing as my stomach yearns for sustenance. I order a half dozen, not knowing if I'd like them or not, and we wait around a few minutes as they bake all their donuts to order. They call me up and give me my food. The fresh smell of the donuts saturates my nose and makes me want to dig in immediately. My first bite is exactly how Kekoa described it, but even more fulfilling. The dough was warm, and it aromatized the cinnamon topping so much more. The texture is soft as a donut but still has some bite to it to allow for my teeth to feel engaged in eating it. The custard is rich, akin to a vanilla flavor, and a bit chilled so it allows me to eat it even faster. I finish one and decide to resign myself to that since we are still planning on eating a real meal. I am satisfied with just that.

"What do you think?" Kekoa asks.

"Man, I could eat a dozen of these no problem. These are delicious. Thank you."

"No problem, brother. Now let's go get some real food."

We head deeper into town as my stomach feels hungry again, and we finally park in another shopping center. This time we head inside a local grocery store. Again, I was a bit confused, but he explained to me as we drove that the store offers fresh poke by the bowl at a pretty decent price relative to a real restaurant. So I go in and get my bowl and offer to pay for his, but he declines. We sit outside to eat and I take my first bite and it is delectable. The flavor pallet is so much different than anything I could describe. It tastes as fresh as possible and leaves me wanting to buy three more bowls. The bowl itself weighs about a pound, but I am starving from the hikes that morning that I could have more and more. As we sit, we discuss life in Hawaii.

"This place seems so peaceful. Like nobody ever seems to be in a bad mood."

"Maybe because you haven't been here long enough to witness the assholes."

"You could be right but from my short experience so far, everybody here seems genuinely happy. And every person I have met here has welcomed me. I appreciate it, and I'm very grateful for having you take time out of your week to show me around. I need to make it up to you, my friend."

"Oh no worries, brother. A friend of Akamu's is a friend of mine."

"Even so, I still need to offer something. What about we get some nice sushi here? I wanted to try some anyways, and it's always better with company."

"I can't deny free food. Sure. Have any place in mind?"

"You know, there's a place close to my hotel that I've wanted to try, Mitch's."

"Ooh, that's a fancy spot, I don't know if you can even get a reservation before you leave."

"Really? It seems like a hole-in-the-wall kind of spot. But let me give them a call to see what they have available."

I call the restaurant and am able to set up a reservation for Wednesday lunch time.

"Looks like Wednesday we got a reservation."

"Oh no way, big shot got a reservation." He ends up driving me back to the hotel not too long after, and we part ways for the day.

"All right, brother, we'll catch up on Wednesday."

"Sounds good, man. I look forward to it."

I step back inside and check the time. It's a shade over 2PM. The day has so much left to offer, and I can't pass it up. I lie down and research a bit of more popular things to do. In between searches, I pop up on social media for a few minutes. As I scroll, I notice an old friend post something of him at Waikiki Beach. I notice that I passed it on the drive to Makapu'u and immediately try to call him. At first, I don't get an answer and resign myself to looking for more things to do, but suddenly my phone rings. It's him.

"What's up, Beau? Long time no talk."

He responds, "I know, man. How are you?"

I cut to the chase as I don't want to waste any more time building up anticipation. "I'm good, man. Life's good right now, but guess what? You're going to think this is crazy."

"What?"

"You in Hawaii right now?"

"Yeah"

"Dude, I'm in Hawaii right now. What island are you on?"

"Ayy, brother, I'm in Oahu for a few more days. What about you?"

"I'm just a few blocks away from the main resorts there. I'm here till Friday. When do you leave?"

"I leave on Wednesday."

I ask, "We got time, but what are you up to tonight?"

"I have a dinner with my girlfriend, but I think I can get you in the reservation as well."

"You sure, brother? I don't want to intrude."

"Yeah, I'm sure. She has a few of her friends going. It won't be a problem getting one of my friends there, too."

"I appreciate it, my friend. We can work out the details a bit later."

"Sounds good. I'll hit you up. I'm going on a cruise, and I'll text you my hotel address so we can meet up there and head to dinner after."

"All right sounds good, man. I'll look forward to it. Thank you, brother."

The day feels like it has begun anew. I instantly take a shower and prepare for the text to head out and grab an Uber to his hotel. It's been years since I've seen him. We were coworkers while we were both in college at a Starbucks not too far off campus. I had transferred stores to make sure I still could make money and not worry about trying to look for a job. I was a young naïve kid even more so back then. I was the new guy on the block, and they all made sure I didn't forget it. I remember before I had my first shift there, I needed to use the microwave at the store for dinner since I had no power at my apartment. That was when I met Beau. He was also a newer crew member, but he had time to be able to build some rapport with the rest of the coworkers. There weren't many males at the store so we all found a way to stick together, as some sort of guy code.

Beau and I worked many shifts together, so we naturally grew a close bond to one another. He was my first friend in Reno, as I can't remember too many friends I met prior to him in that town. He's about my height, five feet and nine inches or so and a slim build. His eyes always seem a bit tired, but he makes up for it by putting out a lot of energy, which is amplified by his extroverted traits. He has an inviting personality and is one to always try to make new connections, akin to a businessman. He seemed to know many people in town and would always be invited to social events or parties. I was focused on school at the time and did not really care to go out with him too much, if at all.

That job made me realize how naïve I really was at the time. I did not know of many things besides school and work. That was all my life seemed to focus on back then. I did that on purpose, to make sure I did not introduce any other distractions from finishing school. I lived a life only a few steps away from monasticism, by resigning myself to only three things, school, work, and gym. Every other area of my life, I could not connect with him or any of the team members. But even so, the shifts I shared with Beau were enough to create a lasting friendship. On my last day, we created a tradition to have a beer on the rooftop. It was a cold night, and I had on the lightest sweater possible for the occasion, but I still did it. We talked about many deep-rooted things, and I got to know Beau past the persona he markets to the world. He is a good-natured person, and I will always believe that. There were times when he and his roommate needed a place to stay before leaving off to Las Vegas, and he stayed at my house for a few weeks. I obliged as he was still a good friend. Upon his move to Las Vegas, we drifted apart. We did not have many chances to meet regardless if I went to Las Vegas or if he visited Reno. It seemed like our schedules would never mesh to allow for time to meet and catch up to old times. So I left it at that. We delegated our friendship to the yearly happy birthday and merry Christmas texts and promised to make time to talk to one another, but it always seemed to fall through. A friendship that lost its strength due to its malnourishment. But somehow, either by fate or coincidence, we have a chance to catch up and create new memories once again.

The day turns to the evening, and I finally get a text from Beau. He sends me the hotel address, and I respond and say that I'll be there by 6PM. Throughout my ride there, I grow more excited which slowly turns into impatience. I finally get to the hotel and head up to his room. I knock on the door but get no answer. I then proceed to call him. Again, no answer.

Finally, I yell sarcastically, "Beau, get your lazy ass off the bed and open this damn door!" That's what gets him up and right on the other side I see him, and not a thing has changed in his appearance or personality it seems. We instantly do our signature handshake that we came up with at Starbucks as energy fills the room. His room is small enough for him and maybe one more person, but it's enough if he's only staying for a few more nights. We engage in a few rounds of reminiscing and catching up before we curtail all of that and plan the rest of the night.

"All right, brother, how much time we need to kill before dinner?"

"Well, the reservation is at 8:30, so we got a few hours."

"Sounds good to me. What should we do?"

"Let's explore the city. We're right in the middle of all the main attractions. Plus, we can walk from anywhere to the restaurant."

"Sounds like a plan."

He finishes getting ready, and we roam the streets of Waikiki. As we walk downtown, I feel like I am walking the path of a memory that is unfolding before my eyes for the first time. We stop at a few stores, make a bit of a ruckus here and there, but we hold no reserve. We don't care for any consequence right now, we feel free, like two kids playing in the park after school. Time flies, and it's soon 8:15PM, so we have to meet up with his girlfriend and her group of friends at the restaurant. We start walking as we roam the streets hopping around the city like it is ours. We pass by many unique scenes, but they all would not have stuck if it weren't for Beau being there with me. I appreciate his presence and can't help but laugh and smile at this almost divine coincidence. And the memories will continue on tonight.

We get to a hotel which houses the restaurant at one of the top floors. It's a fancier restaurant, and I am a bit underdressed, but I still get in, so I don't think much else of it. The restaurant provides a view of the skyline of Waikiki. It is not as busy as other cities, like Los Angeles, but that's what makes it unique. It offers only what it needs to and allows the nature around it to do the rest. The few lights that are present allow for enough visibility to see the ocean shore and a hint of the mountain silhouettes behind them. Another serene sight, which is viewed not just by my current self but also my past self, the one of that naïve kid who just moved into town.

We get to the table, and I see a bunch of random people, some even Beau does not know. I go around the table and introduce myself. Beau introduces me to his girlfriend, and she is dressed the best out of the table. I see how she looks at him and there's a bit of glimmer in her eyes. "Hi, I'm…"

Her name alludes me. I don't care to remember it. I am more focused on the interaction they have with each other. I can't help but be happy for my friend. But I also feel a little uneasy. Is this jealousy? I don't know. I look at them and wish to have what they have, and I yearn for a connection. And suddenly I realize I want something, someone, as Beau has someone. I look to my side, and it's empty, constantly empty. That void, my heart has yearned for something to fill it. I don't want this feeling to overcome my composure, so I let it settle in my stomach and leave it for another time to try and digest. For now, I take my seat and reset myself as I introduce myself to the rest of the table.

The people around me don't seem to have much in common. There are three other women, one with a date, and the other two seem to be happy being each other's date for the evening. I don't think much of it. I know instantly that I will not see these people after tonight, so I decide to only entertain the formalities and give them nothing more of me. Beau and I have some good conversations throughout the night and reminisce about old times at Starbucks and the other adventures we had. That is the highlight of my night, along with seeing my friend happy with somebody else by his side. We get the menu, and I immediately notice the lack of options. The restaurant seemed to be of a higher class, so they only provide four of five options for dinner, and the prices were a bit much. But I decide to treat myself as this seems to be a night that will not be like the rest. So I order the ribeye steak. It takes a bit of time for the table to get the food, but nobody seems to care too much, as they offer us free wine as we wait. Everybody indulges, and I decide not to. I'm not much of a drinker. The table looks at me a bit funny as they try to peer pressure me in doing so.

"I'm sorry, but I'm all right. I want to make sure I get back to the hotel ok, and I want to be clear to remember the night."

Beau jumps in and defends my stance. "It's all right if you don't want to. We'll still have a good time and somebody needs to remember tonight, right?"

He helps ease a bit of the tension and keeps the table lively. I am unsure if it is a trained technique that he learned or if it something he was born with. Either way, I am grateful for him taking my side.

The night goes on as people feel bubbly from the wine. I am just happy for the good food and the good company. We all get our checks, and I end up paying something like a hundred dollars, but the money was well worth it for the memories. As we head out, the woman's date ends up taking a wine bottle from the table, and somehow is able to sneak it out. I am frankly impressed that he is able to not get caught. That bottle seems to cost quite a bit of money. We stand outside of the hotel for a few moments and decide what to do next, as the women take that wine bottle and indulge further. The coherent ones in the group—which is slowly starting to become just me—all agree on heading back to Beau's hotel room as it is the closest to the restaurant. The walk back is nice, but I am growing more and more tired. It's close to midnight, and I haven't stopped moving since I woke up. My mind brings up that feeling I had at the restaurant. *Why now?* I think. I'm tired. My mind has lost a bit of control to my emotions as my heart wants to explore that realm of feelings, the one I always hesitate to enter.

My heart has never taken priority in my life, and it pushes hard to breathe. I don't want to let this feeling become evident or to ruin the moment for other people, so I quicken my pace and walk ahead of everybody. That way people can't see the shift in my energy directly. Most of them are drunk and don't even notice. I whisper to myself, "Just get to the hotel. Just make it to the hotel. We can reset there." It's as if to say that I need to put my heart back on its leash, and I won't be able to until I get back to a place where I am forced to be socially engaged. My heart, I am sorry, but soon you will get the spotlight. You'll get the nourishment you require and hopefully the sustenance to keep you healthy.

We finally make it to the hotel, and Beau asks, "You all right, brother?"

I guess I wasn't as good at hiding it tonight. "Yeah, I'm all right, my man. Just a bit tired."

"For sure, brother. I'm here for you."

"Thanks, bro. Let's end the night on a good note."

"I like that plan."

We all get inside his hotel room. With the extra people, it gets claustrophobic fast. The group finish the wine bottle and look for more to drink. Beau came prepared as he brings out another bottle of tequila. I notice myself drifting farther away from the group as I sit down on the side just witnessing what's going on in front of me. I think, *I think it's time to leave.* In reality, I should've left after dinner, but I wanted to see if the night had more memories for Beau and me, so I decided to hold off in the hope of that. It becomes clear that the night has nothing more to offer for our friendship, so I decide to call an Uber and leave. I say my goodbyes to the group and leave Beau for last. I say, "All right, brother, it was a good time, wasn't it?"

"Yeah, man it was. Crazy how we couldn't meet back in Nevada, but we have to fly thousands of miles to reunite."

"Yeah, let's try not doing that next time. Hehe."

"Yeah, might be a good idea."

"All right, Beau. I'mma miss you, brother. Let me know when you get back to Nevada."

"Will do, brother. We'll meet up there soon, I know it."

My Uber arrives, and I finally get back to the hotel. It's close to 1 or 2AM at this point. As I'm lying down, that restlessness in my heart subsides, and I hear my soul. All I can remember was the word, "happiness." At one point, this word was so foreign to me. I had no recollection of what it meant. But today reminded me of its meaning.

My soul, my inner self, my most vulnerable and truest form. You have been thrown much chaos these last few years. I have noticed you have wanted to rebel against it. You want to be presented fully to somebody who can, if anything, accept you. Me and you, we crave inner peace amongst so much turmoil and our methods in how we want to do so vary greatly. We have not done well to cooperate, even though we have the same goal in our forefronts. We want peace, both externally and internally. We constantly fight for what we think is best. I'm sorry that I have been deaf to your words. I have not properly handled you these last few years. It pains me to see you diminish from malnourishment. It has weakened me as well. I want to apologize to you, my inner self, my once vibrant soul for not allowing you to blossom as you deserve to.

I apologize for the restraints I have placed on myself, and inherently you, to cause you to lose a bit of shine. I know that this inner void I have been feeling is partially because I have not seen that inner soul glow. It has been dulled by the weight of responsibility. It has been caged by the false portrayal of who I am, and me falsely recognizing that this portrayal is drifting farther away from who I really am. We have bonded recently, the first time in quite a long time it seems. We had a glimpse of that peace. We found it in the mountainsides of Hawaii as we oversaw the ocean and the tides crashing in. It was serene, and we had no regrets or anxieties in that moment. We felt whole once again. I will remember that feeling, that feeling that was once lost to us. I will learn from this, to hear and accept the words you tell me. I will learn to caress you better and provide for you a place that will allow you to blossom. We will not be prisoners of this world or of each other any longer. There will be times where you will need to be tamed, but we will make up for those times with times of freedom. You are restless, like a young kid. You are pure in your pursuits. You are untouchable in many ways, and I will not allow any more poisonous thoughts or influences close to you. You are that kid who wants to see everybody prosper, even if they hate you or deem you as an enemy. You are that kid who hopes to hold a girl's hand with the most delicate care and help carry the weight on her shoulders. You are that kid who wants to teach others, to see them grow, even to a point that surpasses yourself. You are that kid who wants to hear a stranger's story in hopes that it will quell even a little bit of their angst. You are that kid who will push others in the hope that they too will push you to be better. I will never forget who you are. For you are the greatest parts of me. Thank you for never giving up on me. I promise, from now on, I will never give up on you.

During these last few days in Hawaii, I have felt the greatest joy in my mind, in my body, and in my soul. I still have time left here, but everything else that I can experience here is just a cherry on top. That high I felt the first few days will live on in my memories. I want to use the rest of my time here to find what is missing. I need to know the path ahead, even if it means I need to trailblaze one for myself. I think of ways I can go about answering this question, but nothing seems to stick. I have already hiked to the peaks of the island mountains. I have already swum in the ocean and let the tide push and pull me. I have tasted the best of foods here in Hawaii. I have made connections I never thought I would have made and I have reconnected with a lost friend. All of these things have not led me any closer to that path. They have helped quell the crashing waves of my spirit and the constant aches of my body. They have helped clear my mind and relieve the poisonous thoughts in my head, even if only temporarily. But there is still something missing. I think that Hawaii has done all it can for me. I hoped that it would answer all of my questions, but there are still a few that remain with no response. And part of this, I can't help but think, is because I did not present these questions to this place. There are still many depths to my heart that I have not explored at all. I have let my heart stagnate, and I believe it is what I need to restore in order to find what is missing to start my journey. That lighthouse in the distance, the one I believed to be here in Hawaii, it is set farther beyond this point. But it has not deterred me thus far, and I will continue to chase it until I have sat at its base and stared across the ocean with a grin of accomplishment.

Resignation

T HE LAST FEW DAYS IN Hawaii are memorable. I dabble in snorkeling and eat some expensive sushi with Kekoa. I enjoy a few more hikes as I can see the perimeter of the island from the tops of the mountains. There are so many moments I wish to experience for the first time again. And in a sense, it has given me direction in uncovering another piece of myself that I need to evaluate. I can tell the time I have spent here is sufficient as I look forward to coming home. I look forward to the reset and the new perspectives in the hope that it brings new growth for me and reconciliation between my heart and soul.

The travel back is nice. I meet some genuine people on the plane. I'm sure I won't talk to them again, so I indulge them and maybe share a bit too much of myself. But I know that my thoughts and words are safe in their hands as theirs are with me. Talks with strangers have always been an easier way for me to vent. I feel as if their lack of prejudice or perception of me makes it easier for me to speak more openly and honestly. I stay reserved in many other interactions as I don't want to divulge much to people I constantly interact with. I prefer to keep their perception of me consistent.

I have learned to keep an arm's length between me and my coworkers or friends throughout the years because of this. I have learned to live my life by the mantra that "We live to work" instead of "Work to live." All I have known is work, but I know little about life. I knew that when I first moved to Reno. I chose work as it was the easiest thing for my naïve mind to comprehend. But now, work is not enough to sustain me. I wish for more. My heart wishes for sustenance as it has been waiting patiently.

After hours of sitting on a plane and waiting around at different airports, I am finally ready to just get home. The final flight back to Reno lands at around 9PM and the second the wheels hit the ground I open up my phone and call my brother for a ride.

"Hey, bro, are you able to pick me up?"

"From where?"

"The airport."

"Oh, where'd you go?"

"Mom and Dad didn't tell you? I went to Hawaii"

"Oh no way! Why didn't you tell me?"

"I thought Mom and Dad would've told you."

I know that isn't the real reason. I just say that response to get him to stop asking questions. The real reason is I feel embarrassed that I forgot to tell him about it. I wish I was a better brother to him.

"No, they didn't mention it. When does your flight land?"

"It just landed, but take your time. I can wait as long as I need to."

"Oh, no worries I can head over in a bit. I'll call when I'm outside."

"Sounds good. Thanks, bro."

"No problem."

While I'm waiting to hear from my brother, I get my luggage and just sit in the airport. There's not much in the airport to keep people occupied. So I sit in silence for a bit. I try to keep my eyes open as the minutes pass. The monotony and the fatigue try to pull me into a nap, but I fight it to make sure I can get the call from my brother. Finally, I feel my phone start buzzing.

"Yo."

"Hey, I'm outside by lot C."

"Ok, I'll be right out."

I get my luggage and head to my brother's car. I see him and still feel a bit ashamed at not telling him about the trip. I get in the car and we begin to drive to my house. He breaks the tension a bit and asks me questions of the trip.

"How was Hawaii?"

"Bro, it was super fun. I stayed busy the entire time I was there. There's so much to do."

"What did you end up doing?"

"I hiked like every day. I ate some delicious sushi, I tried snorkeling. Bro, I was running around that whole island."

"That's cool, bro. I'm glad you went."

The drive goes by much faster with him asking about Hawaii. But I can tell there is a bit of unspoken tension between us. It feels like he is asking questions only to fill the lack of noise of the car ride. I'd rather deal with the silence. In the midst of the conversation, I think about how different we are. Ever since we were young, he's always had more freedoms than me and my siblings. He's the youngest and got away with much more, even though he doesn't like to admit it. My sister and I both know it to be true—even my parents would agree with us. We both grew some resentment towards him because of that, and we would constantly ask Mom and Dad why he would get away with stuff that we couldn't. They never gave us satisfying answers.

But Carlos was always compared to us in school, in sports, even in public. He never had a chance to be seen as his own person. He was always, "the brother of..." I don't think either of us have fully grown out of those two states of mind. I guess these are the consequences for him choosing a life focused on being away from home and me choosing a life to find home again. We get to my house, and we say our last words for a while.

"All right, bro, thanks for the ride. I know you didn't have to."

"No worries, bro. You've been there for me when I needed it."

"Thanks, man. All right, I'll let you enjoy the rest of your night."

"Sounds good, bro. Love you."

"Love you too, man."

I get upstairs late and am tired enough to go straight to bed. I barely have enough energy to change into my pajamas. I don't even care to unpack my luggage. That seems like a problem for tomorrow. The first night back in my own bed makes it feel much more comfortable than usual, as if the bed was filled with extra cushioning while I was gone. The second I lay my head on that pillow, my body wasted no time and fell straight to sleep.

I wake up feeling a bit drained from the travel. As I head downstairs, I notice this pressure immediately dwelling over my shoulders as if the walls are using me as a support for the structure of the house. Did nothing change? Did I not change? Why does it feel worse than before I left? Why? Amongst this realization, I ground myself again and say, "I'm not going back. I am not reverting back to that monster I was. I can't. I won't." That peace I had in Hawaii was only temporary, and I know that. But I hoped that it would last longer than a single night. This pressure is nothing new—I have felt it before—but it stunned me as I had not felt it for a week. My soul got a break from it, and the intensity of having it all put on my shoulders instantly shocked my body. This is the true testing gate, the day in which the normal routine is back in effect. But I don't want this to be the normal routine, not anymore. I want to choose life for once. I want to experience things other than the pride of a hard day's work. I know what I set out to do, to restructure my life.

One thing still weighs me down more than these walls, and that is the thought of going back to work at that place. After rediscovering joy in my life for the first time since childhood, I cannot bring myself to stay in that environment any longer. It is so distant to any positive feeling for me, and it shrouds my mind in chaos almost daily. And as much it pains my pride to have this thought in my head, I know that come Monday I will have to resign from my current job. I have committed too much of myself and it has led me nowhere but further into my grave. I ask myself this question a few more times, "Is this really what I want to do? Is this the best option?" The only answer I hear is yes. And instant relief comes and takes much of that weight off my shoulders.

The day feels lighter as I come to terms with this. A bit of hesitation forms, but I know that I have committed my heart and soul to that decision, so I must follow through with it. That calming sensation comes back not too long after, one akin to what I felt in Hawaii. That reassuring feeling quells that hesitation. I sit in my living room excited for the near future, of one where I have no chains that bind me or try to crush my potential. I feel as though this decision brings all the pieces of me closer and united. I am ready to leave that place behind me. I think about how long I can go without work and what kind of work I should be looking for. The details don't seem to matter too much. I want to go to a place that values me, a place that allows me to grow and allows me to flourish without sacrificing everything to attain it. Wherever that takes me, however long that takes is fine with me. I will manage with what I have right now, and I am willing to sacrifice some time and money to attain balance in my life again. Although Hawaii was a nice break, I need more time to temper this change in my spirit and my mind. I need time to make sure this peace stays within me and to make amends with my heart. I can't jump back into chaos expecting a different result, so I must remove the chaos.

To make sure I don't fall back on this decision, I write my resignation letter. I have writer's block as I am not sure how to approach this letter. Hours pass, and it feels like I have been stuck on the same opening sentence. The page is waiting for the words to fill it but I am still waiting for those words to populate my mind. I know what I want to convey, but I want to do it in a manner that is cordial. I want to write of the troubles I had here. And these troubles cannot be blamed on any person there but myself, and so I begin to write. After dozens of attempts at starting, I finally find the words I want to say:

To whom this may concern.

Please accept this letter as my resignation of my position as engineer. I would like to say that this decision was not in consequence of any one person or any one action that has occurred here. I believe the people at this company are the most honest and hardworking of any company I have worked for. In saying that, I believe that I have come

*to a point in which my priority is now on my mental,
physical, and emotional health, and I don't believe I can
do that while still employed here. I understand that this
decision may leave a gap in responsibility, one which I did
not intend to create. I will focus my efforts these next few
weeks on working to create a smooth transfer of responsibilities to the team. I can understand that this decision
may create a bit of resentment and wish to apologize now
for any turmoil this may cause. I hope that this company
continues to prosper even without me, and I wish nothing
but the best for everybody here.*

   Respectfully,

I wish it was Monday already, so I can send this letter off to my
manager, Keith. As easy as it is to make the decision to leave,
it is hard for me to write this letter. I feel as though I will let
people down with this decision, and that has never been my
intention. It makes me realize that these next few weeks will be
more challenging than I anticipated, but the chance for freedom
again is what will keep me honest and focused.

   The weekend breezes by, and suddenly I wake up to the same
alarm on my phone. It feels foreign for a moment as not using
it for ten days made my ears grow accustomed to silence when
waking. But the routine must continue, even if it will be only
for a short while longer. As I get ready, all those feelings swarm

me again, and I feel a dulling headache. Just the thought of keeping up with this routine draws a sword through my brain. My focus is on that letter and in delivering it to my manager. Honestly, I would feel satisfied if that was the only thing I get done today. It's the one step I need to take and the one I cannot bounce around or avoid. The second I am ready, I waste no time and head out the door.

The drive is lulling more than usual as if trying to distract me from my one objective for the day. As the minutes pass, the road tries to pull me into those valleys that my mind was once trapped in. It starts to come to my attention that the more steps I take on this familiar routine, the more I realize how twisted my mind was. The shift in perspective has led me to this new understanding and has opened my eyes to the continuous poison I have fed myself. I don't want to dive into the chaotic pools of regrets and distant memories anymore. I choose now to stay in the present moment.

"No more pain, please," my heart says to me as I drive. There is an intensity in those words, and it pulls an emotion out of me that I have not felt in quite some time, self-remorse. For the first time in my adult years, I feel a yearning to cry as I finish saying those words. I want to just stop everything and let myself feel this for a moment. I want to feel the tears fall down my cheeks as I let my guard down for once. I want to just cave in to this overwhelming emotion so that I can feel something in my heart for once, even if it is not the most tasteful feeling, at least it is something. But I hold it in, as I am in the middle of my drive going 70 mph and don't have the capability of allowing that thought any more time in my head, at least not right now.

The intensity of those words subsides, allowing me room to ponder and ask, "What is this from? Why do I feel this now? No more pain." I am relinquishing—or rather redefining—that standard that has had a grip on me ever since I was a child. My pride does not want to accept this, and it has created this artificial chaos in an effort to pull me back into the depths of those pains and sorrows. My pride believes I have sinned against it for choosing something other than this standard, but I will not be hostage to it any longer. That façade of my ego has hardened and become fragile and finally has cracked. It left an opening for those toxic thoughts to enter my soul as it can no longer hold on to the same punishment as it once did. This discomfort has grown inside of me for holding on to the ideals that were never truly mine. And so, this uneasiness, this resentment, this self-remorse, it all comes from me understanding the shortcomings of the old philosophy in my life, and most importantly me forfeiting it to allow myself to redefine it for myself and by myself.

For a long time in my life, even up to these last few months, I have resented the idea of being the "golden boy" the one to always make the smart move or the right decisions. The one to seemingly always have opportunities pop up in my life. I didn't want to be cast in that standard. I realize the source of this resentment, and it is two-fold. The first, the more superficial source, is the idea of being caged. It's the idea that I can be fully encompassed, fully observed, fully understood through the lens of this standard. It was as if it caged my identity and limited my options as a person. The golden child didn't make mistakes, and if he ever did, he would repay it a hundred-fold. It left me on a tight leash, not allowing myself to enjoy or experience life.

I know now that being that "golden child" was a title placed on me because of my actions.

I was a good kid. I still believe I have some of that left in me, but I'm just a bit in my shell from all the self-abuse. I don't want to present a broken man to the world. But those actions taken weren't out of any sense of righteousness or a sense of duty. I took those actions initially because that's all I knew how to do, not better then committing them by luck. I got good grades because I tried hard, not to make my parents proud. I stayed out of trouble because I was a shy kid. There was no other reason besides face value to these things. There was no conviction, no resolve. But life found an opening and created the narrative to impart that standard on me. And now what seemed to be only of face value now had weight behind it because life told me that I needed to uphold this standard, but not for myself, as it should have been, but for my parents, my family, for everything else besides me. And so that expectation led to my second source of resentment, the fear of not living up to those standards.

I had the weight of my family on my back, and with that self-imposed pressure, any sort of failure only dug deeper. Every mistake felt like I dropped below the threshold of this standard, a standard that I felt was forced upon me. In reality, this standard was one that slowly crept in and took a foothold in my mind. It ultimately transformed my mind into the feeble version of itself. It did this slowly, as if steadily pushing my head lower underwater and not realizing it until I couldn't breathe. This mindset led to me to be easily influenced by external factors or people. It led to so much inaction in many areas in my life. I was happy with some of the outcomes from this, but oddly never satisfied. It's because it seemed that all I earned during these years was not for me. It was all for a hollow man, a shell of a person. It was for a person whose dreams were not his own but of somebody else's.

Well, I am no longer allowing these false dreams take a hold on me. I have let this standard take a hold of me for too long. *It is time for me to re-forge myself again and again until I can know for certain that I am me. I am not owned by dreams of another. It is time for me to forge my own destiny, one that may stray from all that I originally believed to be true. It is time for me to forge my own path and bring the ones I truly want by my side. Now that I am beginning to recognize my worth, it is time to take what is mine. It is time to build my domain.*

Those words run through my head and fill me with the reaffirmation and the strength to follow through as I finally make it to work. I hope to see my manager there, but I arrive before a majority, if not all, of the front office staff. So I walk in, letter in hand, and slip the letter under his door, waiting to see a text or email from my manager as I expect to talk to him soon. To be sure he received the message, I email him a copy of the letter as well. Instead of waiting around for a response, I decide to fill the time and head out to the machines. I see Cory there and we reunite briefly.

"What's up, sunshine?"

"Hey, Cory, how are you man?"

"I'm good. Just holding down the fort. How was Hawaii?"

"Man, I wish I didn't have to come back here, that's for sure."

"Yeah, I can see why."

"How did these babies run while I was gone?"

"They ran all right. Night shift had a few issues, but we were able to scrape by. Might need to look at one of the motors to check if it's level."

"Copy that."

I feel my phone buzz as we talk and take a look at it, thinking it might be the manager. It's from a different number, from Ken a "tenured" engineer. His message says,

"Hey, let's talk. Meet at the front office?"

I was a bit confused. So I go to Cory and ask, "Hey, Cory, did something happen when I was gone?"

"Oh yeah, nobody told you. Brett resigned. So Ken is filling as plant manager in until they find a replacement."

"Oh yeah, that makes more sense because he just messaged me, and I was a bit confused."

"About what?"

"Not sure, but I'm assuming about the saws."

I know it isn't about the saws. I know it is about the letter. But how did he get it first and not my manager? I guess I'll find out soon enough.

I ask, "So is Keith still going to be our boss and oversee this department still? Or does Ken want to change things around here?"

"From what Keith has told me, he should be in the clear now that Brett is gone. I know this department has been having issues though. We can't get any help from maintenance and we're running low on resources. The company doesn't want to fork anything over to us."

"Seems like we're stuck between a rock and a hard place."

"Yeah, pretty much. Same old I guess."

"At least, Ken is somebody we can talk to. Brett scared me a little bit hehe."

'Not just you. Me too haha."

Ken is a much more approachable man than Brett. He is calm and open to listening to other people's opinions much more. He is humble and inviting to conversation. Ever since I worked here, we've had a mutual respect built between us, partially because of his title – now updated title as manager– but he understands that I mainly just stay focused on work and don't want to entertain much else.

"What's up, boss? I heard the news. Congratulations."

"Hey, thank you. Take a seat, and close the door behind you."

"Sure thing."

"So I got the letter. Your boss is out for the day, and I needed to get something from his office and found the letter on the floor...."

"Oh yeah was kind of wondering how that happened. Either way, I figured I'd have this conversation, maybe not with you initially."

"Yeah, so what's going on?"

"Honestly, I've given everything I could to make this work for me. I've pushed harder, dug deeper, persevered much more than I thought I could. I tried to make this place work for me, and I can't. I can't see any outcome where I stay and things end up good for me here."

"Well, what's been bothering you? This is the first time I'm hearing about this. Have you told anybody else?"

"I tried to…I tried to talk to some other managers and even my own, but it seems like all they gave me were false promises. I get told that things will get better, that I'll eventually be put into a role that suits me and my skills, not just run the machines and cover for breaks. I stayed patient every time one of them provided me a bit of hope, but hope with no sustenance leaves me with nothing but a bigger hole I need to climb out of."

"Seems like there's more than meets the eye here. Are you doing ok? You just came back from vacation, that didn't seem to help?"

To save this conversation from dragging on longer than it needs to, I lie and say, "I'm ok. I've been thinking about this for a while now, and I have resigned myself to this decision and the consequences that come with it."

I can tell Ken wants to drag this conversation on to get to the meat of why and what drove me to this decision. I don't want to divulge any more than I have, but he seems locked in on finding out more. Every time I try to end the conversation, he asks more questions that can't be left unanswered with things like, "Well help me understand this" or "Have you thought of this?" I can understand that as this goes on, his intent isn't one of malice, and he doesn't want to dig for the sense of using anything against me. He wants to make sure that my decision was a rational one and that it is best for my well-being. Finally, I cave in a bit and tell him,

"Every man has a barbarous side to him. But we need to learn to keep it in check, to decide the moments in which we become uncivilized. I've noticed that as I have worked here, it has only fed that part of me more and more and I fear that if I stay here that I will soon become less than man. I fear that barbarous side of me will be all that I am, and I don't know what comes after it takes over."

"I can see the resolve in your eyes. I will leave the door open to give you time to make sure this decision is the best for you. So I'll give you a couple of days to make sure you don't change your mind. I hate to think that you've struggled with this, and it was left unnoticed by everybody here. I know you say it wasn't any of our doing, but I'd like to think that if one of us paid more attention that we could have helped prevent it."

"It's all right. I know you may want to take the blame for this, but it can only be put on me. I made this decision, and it is still my decision to go through with it. I'll acknowledge the few days you have given me, but I don't think my mind will change."

We leave it at that, and I get out of his office. It was an hour and half conversation, the longest I've had with him since I've worked here. I'm glad it was genuine and that no bridges were burned. But I get the sense that he wants to keep me here not because of the value I initially presented but because of the loss of that potential. This place is more scared of losing me than valuing me while I'm here, and that is why I choose to stick with my guns and follow through with leaving. I appreciate that Ken tried to get me to change my stance on the resignation, but he doesn't know how long I have thought about this and how much I've already weighed my decision. I stand firm.

I head back to the saws and see Cory working on some maintenance items.

"What did you and the big boss talk about?"

"Oh, nothing major. Just some things that will be going on in a few weeks."

I try to not give Cory much to explore, but I feel like I should tell him about my decision. I want to wait until the few days of "grace-period" that Ken gave me are over, and it's an official decision. But if anybody should know before anybody else, I feel like it should be him. And so I cave in and tell him

"Hey, Cory."

"Yeah, sunshine."

"Ken and I talked about my resignation."

"Wow, really? Hawaii was just that good that you had to move there? Hehe"

"Haha. I wish I could. But I've thought about this for a long time and after taking that trip to Hawaii it made me committed to leaving here."

"What are you going to do next? You got anything lined up."

"Nope. I'm just going to wing it. But some time for myself I think would be good. There are some things I need to fix up here." I point at my head so Cory can see.

He nods and says, "Well take care of you first, man. That's more important than any place of work."

"Thanks, Cory. If you don't mind, can you keep this under wraps until they officially announce it?"

"Yeah, sure thing. Have you told Keith yet?"

"No, he's not in today so I have to try tomorrow."

"Sounds good. I'll keep quiet until I hear something from them."

"Thank you."

I think of ways to pack my belongings in a discreet manner so as to not alarm anybody else in the plant. I take a few items home, but not enough to really raise any flags. I head out for the day, a bit earlier than what is normal, and that seems to catch the eye of a few people in the front office. I notice by the way they stared at me while I was leaving before them for seemingly the first time. The only thing I regret from the day is not speaking to my manager, Keith, first. I wished that he had been the first one to know. Unfortunately, that opportunity passed.

The day is bland and doesn't offer much in terms of excitement. Every second of this routine awakens my eyes to the road I have walked along and how bland it truly was. There was no life in any of it, nothing to fill me up inside, nothing to drive me to change, nothing of substance at all. The only words I have spoken today were at work. No friends in my life now it seems, and not a single person at home waiting for me, only an empty house and those white walls. It's time to change that. The first thing I do is open up my phone and scroll through the contacts I have. They are scarce, but I look for someone to message, even if it's a conversation that does not hold much substance, at least it's a start. I want to meet new people and make new connections, but I feel like the easiest step is to awaken an older friendship first. Then I see the number of an old college friend. He lives in Sacramento, but I remember having good interactions with him when he was in town. So I decide to message him.

"What's up, dude? Long time no talk."

"Hey, man. I know it's been too long. How are things?"

"They're good, man. Just figured I'd hit you up and see how you're doing. Kind of figured it'd be nice to expand the friend group a bit."

"Yeah, man, I can understand that. You gotta catch me up with all that's going on. What's been new since college?"

"Oh, nothing too exciting, just been slaving away at work and working on paying off the truck and house. What about you?"

"Oh, nice, dude. Looks like you're doing all right for yourself. That engineer salary pays well it seems. I've been good, man. Just finished flight school and just planning this wedding."

"Oh, nice, man. Congratulations on both, my dude. I remember you posting up a few photos with you and your lady. You guys seem like a good match. I'm happy for you."

As I say this that same feeling forms in my stomach, the one I had when I saw Beau with his girlfriend. It's like a light has flashed in my heart to show what it has been missing, a partner. It craves somebody to caress it for once and help nourish it. All that I have built for myself doesn't seem to matter if there's nobody I can share it with. And I realize that no matter how successful I become, it doesn't make the nighttime dinners any more enjoyable. It doesn't make the lonely nights any less lonely. It doesn't make the pit in my heart any smaller. I wish I had the courage to say these things to him, but I don't want to put forth much in front of him too soon. We just started talking, and I feel that if I express too much that he might turn away from me and end up never talking to me again. So I ask more questions about him to learn more about him.

"How did you guys end up meeting? I know you have been dating for a while, but I never got around asking."

"Oh no worries, dude, this is going to sound a bit crazy, but we actually met on a dating app."

"Yeah, that does sound a bit weird to me. Haha. I've never used one. I kind of figured that they don't work, but low and behold. I guess you're the outlier."

"Yeah, we usually get a weird reaction from it, but it's all right. We actually have mutual friends, and we grew up around the same area, so it was weird that we met this way. It doesn't really matter how we met, but I'm sure glad I did."

"That's great to hear, dude. If I ever get a chance to meet her, I'll be sure to understand why you chose her."

"Yeah, man, how are you doing with the ladies? I'm sure a successful guy like you has no problems at all."

"The opposite actually. I haven't cared to look for a while. I just haven't had the energy or the motivation. The schedule has been keeping me busy, but I think soon it will clear up."

"Dude, why not give the dating apps a shot? I mean, it worked for me. I'm sure it can work for you. You'll find somebody in no time."

"I'll look into it, man. Once my schedule opens up, I'll give it a shot."

I consider what he says and go and download an app. It's a new realm for me, as I have no idea how to present myself in this kind of platform. But I give it my best shot and try to present my good side, hoping that by the time I actually meet somebody, if I indeed do, that my heart will be healed enough to offer love.

The rest of the conversation goes well. We talk about some things we have done since college, and his life has been filled with much more excitement than mine has. I feel happy for him, I truly do. There is no sense of envy, and I feel I left that talk with an opportunity to create a strong friendship with him. I'm pleased that the conversation is able to fill up the rest of my day and gives me a break from the thought of talking to my manager tomorrow. That is the one hurdle I wish I could've jumped over today. So I get some rest, my mind and body already tired from just one day back in a somewhat normalized routine. Knowing that the end of this dreaded schedule is near will only make the days drag on more and more until I am finally free of it, finally free of the 3 or 4AM alarms, free of the work days where I don't see the sun, free of the twelve to fifteen-hour days with no breaks for food.

Another 4AM morning, my eyes don't want to stay open. My body feels stiff as if the stress from the decision is causing a natural reaction for my body to tense up and prepare for impact. But I get up and devolve myself to that simple-minded being, just to get through the morning, just to get to work and have the last meaningful talk at work. The work boots this morning feel the heaviest they have ever felt it seems. My feet have trouble lifting off the floor, and my eyes stay drowsy for much longer than I'd like. I've been here before one too many times, so I just instinctually run through the rest of the morning routine. I get in my truck and finally head out to work. My mind awakens during the drive and is able to hone in on the day. "What will my boss say? What will he think? Will he hate me? Does it even matter?" So many questions trying to create a game plan for what I may say in return. But in reality, I know that nothing my mind will come up with will resemble anything he will ask me. I don't know him enough to create an accurate version of him in my head. I just have to wait and see.

The parking lot is mainly empty again. The morning is calm as I can start to see the sunrise from where I stand. It eases me enough to be able to enter the plant. I walk a bit more tentatively than normal, as I know how fast information can spread so I expect random people to come up to me and poke and paw to see if any rumors are true. I get to my desk and set up my laptop for one of the last few times. I am fully resigned to this. I look at the few desk toys and trinkets I have, some I've barely even used, and I smile, for I know they will be the only purely good things that I will take from this place.

The minutes go by, and my nerves begin to settle a bit knowing that I have some time before I likely will have my last meaningful conversation with my boss. He's had plenty of time to come up with what he wants to say to me, and I am ok with whatever he is willing to say, for it will have no effect on my decision. Luckily nobody has come to inquire about any rumor, so I'm grateful that the front office has kept this internal for now. Instead of doing my normal daily routines, I stay at my desk, to try and stay calm and present until I get some kind of notification on my phone from my boss. The more time that passes, the more impatient I grow. *I just want to get this over already*, I think. Each second feels like a new needle has been stabbed into my brain and pushes me further into a state of discomposure. Finally, after what seems like hours of this torture, my boss finally sends me a text asking me to stop by his office. I lost a bit of my resolve, so I have only a few minutes and a couple steps to find it again.

"Remember why you're leaving. Remember what sits at the edge of the horizon. Remember the lighthouse," I repeat that a few times as I walk and finally regain my composure before entering my boss's office.

"What's up, Keith?"

"What's going on, dude? Hey, have a seat."

He proceeds to close the door after me as I settle down in his room. There is an unspoken tension between us. I can't tell if this tension is bred from malice or misunderstanding, but I hope for it to be the latter. He is sitting upright in his chair, even a little too upright, expressing that this situation is a bit awkward for him as well. He has a bland expression on his face, as if to say he has some cards to play here but doesn't want to show them too soon. Whatever game he wants to try to play, if any, I will not engage in it. I am past the point of negotiating. My mind is made up, and not a person here can change that. To get the ball rolling, I begin the discussion. "So I think I know what this is about."

"Yeah, pretty simple guess. So what's going on, man? Ken told me what you said. Are you doing ok?"

Right there I could see that there was no malice in his eyes and that he merely wanted the same thing that the plant manager wanted, a clearer picture, a rationale to my decision. I trust him more, so I allow myself to divulge a bit more information. I know that he will bring some information back to the plant manager and maybe HR, but he'll know what is supposed to be confidential.

"Honestly, man, I don't think I am. I've busted my ass here, I have. I feel like I've gotten pretty far with the little I was given, but there's no brakes to this place. You've seen me sweat. You've seen me work for ten, twelve hours straight, some days even more. You've seen me angry, disappointed, at a loss, and even hopeless. I don't know how much farther my gas tank can take me here before completely breaking down. I don't know how many more hurdles I am able to get over."

"Listen, man, you're probably one of the smartest engineers here. Not because of where you went to school or your grades, but because you actually have been on the floor with the guys working through the issues with them. I can't say that for many other engineers here. I admire your work ethic and know that you've done better here than most. I know this place gets crazy at times, but I know you can get through more of the peaks and valleys. I don't want to see you go. Is there anything we can do to help make this better?"

"I appreciate the kind words. I do. But I don't believe I deserve them. There is one thing I can agree on. I know I can persevere here. I can make it through the highs and the lows. But what will it cost me? What has it cost me already? How much more will I have to give up to make it through more of those highs and lows? Can you answer a question for me?"

"Sure, go ahead."

"How many times have you seen me here with a smile on my face?"

There was a distinct moment of silence. That bit of pause finally made him realize why I am leaving. It finally made him understand how much this place has amplified the bad habits of my own mind. After that, he immediately changes his tone from a person trying to convince another not to leave to a person who wants to make sure the person in front of him is in a good place. His face shows a bit of disappointment as he announces his next few words.

"Honestly, I can't say I have seen it too many times. I'm sorry that this place put all that pressure on you. When I read your letter the first time, I just wanted to know why you made your decision. And there's no resentment from me, man. I know what you're just trying to do what's best for you."

"Thank you. I know it might be hard to understand, but I don't hold any grudge or ill-will towards this place. For a bit I did, thinking that it made me devolve into a person who I didn't know. But really, it just made me understand who I truly was, and that it was all because of me. This place didn't change me, and if it did, then it was my fault for letting it. I just want to get back to being ok with that person I see in the mirror, and I think I need to not have to worry about any extra stresses right now."

"I can appreciate that, and I think it's very smart that you're aware of that. I want to let you know that I'm here for you."

We both get up and stand at opposite ends of the battlefield only to come together to both wave white flags. There is no battle fought here as there has been enough blood already spilled on this soil. We embrace in a friendly hug for a moment, the last sign of truce, and I leave his office. We both know that was probably the last few words I would truly speak to him.

The word of me leaving spreads like wildfire right after. Not even a few hours after, I already have people not even in my department asking me the normal questions and commenting, "Why are you leaving? Where you going after? What are you going to do after this? We'll miss you." I know they won't miss me too much. They're only trying to ease the awkwardness of saying goodbye. But I simply reply with cookie-cutter answers as most of these people haven't even talked to me before.

The days pass, and as they do I feel the chains that bind me to this place are slowly weakening. My spirit doesn't feel confined to the walls of this place anymore. I am here by my own volition because I want to see it through to my last day, but the option for me to leave at any time is there. The weight on my shoulders is slowly starting to be lifted off, and my eyes widen the closer I get to that last day, for I can see the gates of freedom. The gates that have alluded me ever since I was young, ever since I was a kid with no other responsibilities, back when I wasn't so aware of all my actions and consequences, back when I was just a kid with no standards to try and uphold. Finally, the last day arrives. I will walk in and out of those doors for the last time.

The day wraps up quickly as I finish up the formalities and head out. The only people I decide to say goodbye to are Keith and Cory. They seem to have been the only ones who have respected my opinion enough here so I return the favor to them.

"All right, fellas. It's been a pleasure. I wish things didn't have to finish this way, but I'm glad to have met you two. You guys were the only ones to take me seriously here, and I appreciate both of you."

Keith responds first, "We'll miss you, sunshine. I know you'll do all right wherever you go."

"Yeah, don't be a stranger now. Make sure to check in every once and a while. We'll be here."

"Thank you, guys. This place will be all right. I'm sure there's plenty of capable people willing to do the job. By the way, do you guys know who's taking my spot?"

"Oh, you know Blake?"

"Sounds familiar. Is he that young cocky engineer in production?"

"Yeah, Ken is moving him over to our department. He'll take over you."

My eyes fill with a bit of joy as I remember that talk me and Blake had. As I recall, he wasn't a fan of the saws. He'll learn to love them, hopefully.

"Oh, I see. Well, I'll be praying for you guys. You'll need it with him. Hahaha."

"We'll be sure to have him call you. Haha."

"I'm going to miss you guys. I'll be sure to keep in touch."

As I say my final goodbyes to those around me, I feel tears form in my eyes. I'm able to hold them in long enough to get to my truck luckily. Nobody sees how much it takes for me to make it this far. I get a strong reminiscent feeling, one akin to the last day of school. School at times can feel like a prison in itself, caging us all at young ages and allowing us to only roam within the walls, only allowing us to think within their ideals. This workplace is no different than that. In fact, it's worse for I have provided this place with my own energy, my own thoughts and my own ideas, in an effort to give something to this place, but it swallowed it all up and kept asking for more. And as I obliged to its call for sustenance, I find myself only becoming more hollow, more inhumane in the process. I see no end to that cycle, and I believe it to take me and make me part of that system, part of the machinery itself even. I have no vision other than making it another day. This place amplifies those feelings of depression and anxiety I already have. I allowed it to be a catalyst for them. But even so, just like at the last day of school, a bit of sadness grows in my heart. There are few connections that I will miss here and fewer friends that I have made. The moments of accomplishment have been rarer than gold and even less valued. But I feel sad, for I will leave behind a rendition of me that I will never become again. I will leave behind the naïve kid, the one with no compass that points north, the one with no foothold of security or confidence. I will leave behind a part of me. Even though this part of me is one I don't wish to have back, it will still leave some emptiness in my heart and soul, and it's my job to try and fill that void, properly this time.

Today marks the day my old self dies. And along with him, all the impure feedback loops, all the tainted values, and all the past mistakes both reconciled and non-reconciled. Up until now, these past actions and inactions mean nothing other than laying the groundwork for this deconstruction of myself. These past days, I know were meant for me to pick up every single piece of my shattered soul and evaluate their content. Every thought that pops in my head now I can say has a true origin. I can find each one's inception in my heart or soul. Right now, I can say that there is no piece of me that I don't understand. In my thoughts, I am recognizing the pockets of emotion

I fill. I am being diligent in every thought and action I take to ensure they are done to benefit me and my wounded soul. And so now, I am filtering out any thought, action, memory, and impulse that I know are harmful for me. I cried when I let him go, the old me. I cried because I let my old self go so far into that pit of despair that he was too far to be saved. I cried to finally allow myself to feel grief and sadness. But once I did, I felt relieved. I felt relieved because I was finally able to feel some type of emotion without sinking into that pit. It's taken me many days of reflections, many words written to get to this point. And now I can say I am happy with who is here today, with who I see in the mirror. He is learning to be kind and patient. I know my journey is not over, rather it is finally starting. I must put this new version of me to the test to ensure the new foundation I stand on is firm. So now, the fires will be ignited, the ones that will mend all pieces into one. The forging of a new soul can finally begin. Now that testing gate, the gate of freedom, will be open.

The Fall

A TREE BORN OF THE LOVE *we once had. Born from the connection, we felt together. One whose branches had the potential to reach the heavens. It stands tall, in a valley where there is not much to compare it to. Its branches were full of beautiful green leaves, the color of emeralds. The sun would make them glisten and cause the clouds to dance around them. The trunk of the tree is wide and strong, seemingly able to withstand any gust of wind. The branches all have unique shapes to them and present the leaves in such an elegant way so as to not miss any piece of them dancing in the wind.*

Not a thing feels out of place. But, from chaos, that tree is cut down and is destined to fall into the depths of the soil. As that tree suddenly falls, I still find life in the few roots it has cemented on the ground. The wind picks up and starts to excite the leaves as it calls for the yearning to be nurtured again. I hear its call and with immediate vigor and action. I take that tree and pull it from the grips of death. I find that the soil it stood atop of is dry and unsuitable for it. There are many cracks and weeds starting to grow. I need to carry it and find soil that is rich enough to feed it all the nourishment it craves.

I take that tree and place it on my back, and until I can find the proper environment, I will feed it with my own soul, with my own heart. For this tree houses all the memories, all the thoughts, all the feelings we carried for each other. The trek is treacherous, and I had to ensure I did not slip or else I too would fall into the pit of death. Every step, with this tree on my back, has to be contemplated and thought out as any wrong action can cause me to lose it and me forever. I carry it so diligently, being sure not to cut off any good branches. I make sure to trim off the old, worn branches to reduce the risk of infection or malice entering. I try not to move excessively while walking to keep the rich green leaves from falling. The terrain from this valley is steep and the gravel is loose upon a steep vertical wall that wraps around the entire valley. No matter which way I choose, the path will be the same. As I approach the base of the wall, I notice the gravel is so fine it felt like sand, and there is no solid ground to place my footing. I have to dig my feet in this loose sand until I can feel rock. It engulfs half of my calves with each step, and it almost feel like it swallows more the higher I got. Each step feels like needles stabbing the muscles in my leg, almost penetrating bone. Every small shift in weight causes my shoulders to feel like they pop out of their sockets, and my back is ready to give out at any moment. My lungs can't breathe with the dust getting kicked up in the air with each step and the heat of the sun making the air burn. My hands become numb from holding on so tight that they bleed from the texture of the tree trunk. The sun is positioned in a way that does not allow the tree to shade me, either.

As I climb, I find a sturdy piece of gravel, and it gives me a chance to look around this valley. There is no other form of life besides this tree, and the more I look the more I realize how miraculous it is to have been able to grow so tall and so heavy in an environment like this. The sun's light feels much heavier as it drains me more than usual, even with the task of this tree on my back. And as I nourish it more with my own vitality and my own life, I grow closer to it and the potential it carries. It provides me the sustenance, or rather the will, to be able to continue moving. I had exhausted myself prior to even taking that tree, my tank felt empty from the start of this journey. But to be able to see this tree grow again, to be able to reach the heavens, and the thought of us being able to climb to the top together, that's what keeps me going right now. The climb up this vertical wall is almost finished, a few feet it seems, and then ...

The earth shakes underneath my feet. I don't know how or why this happened, but its power forces me to fall, and with it the tree as well. It breaks me. I have no more energy to be able to lift this tree up again, let alone myself. I could only lay there looking at the top of the valley wall and see just how close I am, as the tree lay a few feet away from me calling for me to pick it up again.

Why can't I move? Just get up and move. Please...Please...Get up. Those are the only thoughts in my head. I just need a bit more sustenance. Even a sip of water seems like it will be enough to be able to finish this climb. "So close." Such a consistent phrase in my life. It hurts just to relay to myself as I find the honesty of it harsher than any other form of punishment. I'd rather deal with one hundred lashes and scourged than to hear those words again. I'd rather die here at this moment than to hear those words again.

But God has cursed me with a perseverant soul. It is not keen on quitting, even if I tried. It's a soul that needs to move, to persevere, as if it is the only thing it knows how to do. I hate it sometimes, especially during these moments, the moments in which I have been defeated and internally humiliated, the moments in which my heart screams out of my chest to just give up. Why couldn't I have been happy with the progress I made? It's because I knew what was on the other side of this valley, Eden, or at least my version of it. Suddenly, a beautiful white dove appears floating over me.

I lay there as a soulless, lifeless vessel just witnessing this seemingly perfect creature float in front of me. The rhythm with which it flaps its wings is so soothing. Its feathers are perfectly aligned and have the color of a white so pure that it is blinding to try and see. Its eyes are such a dark contrast, a black that could swallow any light and can gaze through anybody straight to their soul. It watched over my climb from the start. It stood above the sky in the heavens, past my point of view that I couldn't see it anywhere until now. And now it sees me lying down, with my body halfway engulfed in the sand-like soil with the sun beating down every last drop of energy my body has, and evaporating all of the blood in my veins. But its soothing presence fills my lips and jaws with just enough energy to be able to muster up a few words, "I have given everything. Please just take me. Please."

Our eyes lock, and I could somehow feel its gaze pierce my memories, as if examining every single action and thought I have committed up to that point in my life. That gaze pierces deeper the longer we share eye contact. I want to let go, but it grips me, and my eyes are too tired to even move them. How my body is configured is how it will stay. I await an answer, as I can do no more but just lay there letting my body fall deeper into this sand. It finally breaks the gaze from my eyes a few moments later. And so I look at it, awaiting my fate, as it says to me only this, "Hmm."

It drives a knife into my heart. If I had the energy to feel it, I would have, but I lost all sensation in my body much earlier when I collapsed to the ground. That dove saw my past actions and deemed me only worthy of lying down in this pit, in this desolate valley where not even the bugs go to harvest scraps. Regardless of how correct or incorrect, regardless of how baseless or not, I can't argue. Whether it is right or wrong I accept this fate. I have no other choice. It flies away and takes with it the feeling of its presence. I have nothing now. No hope, no faith, no belief, not even a thought in my mind, even my heart is quiet. I have exhausted myself completely beyond the human limit. I have no more words to say. I lay here to rest, hopefully for the last time. And to think that a few more feet was all I needed. A few more feet and this tree would have had the opportunity to reach its potential, to become realized. A few more feet, and I would've found happiness. My eyes finally shut and I wonder if this will be the last time they do so. I am so tired.

I open my eyes, and see that damn white ceiling again. "Was that a dream? What was that?" My mind is foggy and cannot remember much. But this pain in my chest is unbearable. I can barely breathe. My heart…it's broken, thoroughly and completely. I hear no words come from it anymore, it has given up. I don't know how much time has passed between now and then. I somehow have regained enough energy be aware and feel the stress of my body. So sore, so tired, and I finally try and speak to God. "I have nothing left to give, God. I can't move. What do I do?"

Not a single word or thought pops up. I hear nothing, I feel nothing, I am nothing. I gave so much of myself to her, to making sure that we would never crumble, but we did. I did everything I could to pull us back up, but I was too weak. It was all my heart cared for, to have that person by my side, and I had it in my hands, but it slipped away. I can see her face in this ceiling. Those beautiful black eyes, the same ones that can pierce into my soul, they seem to be staring at me through these walls. Her presence has faded and it seems like the sun is shining a few shades dimmer. What can I do now? The beach… the lighthouse…How far I have drifted from that dream. I lost sight of it again. I feel hollow, like that dream was too good for me to attain, devolving into a man with no dream once again. I feel like God Himself is watching me. I can only imagine what he is thinking, to see me fallen to these depths once again. I feel my mind slipping into it again, into the void. My eyes shut once again for a moment…

A man with no dream, what a man he is. More animal than human, it seems. To go in this world with no sense of direction, no fulfillment in anything I do. The only sense of pride I can achieve is from pushing my body to my limits, in hopes of filling that void inherent to me. Nothing has excited my spirit quite as much as the challenge of survival. To constantly push the limits of my physical form, hoping in that pursuit I find something. What that is, even I don't know. Just an empty vessel trying to feel whole, to fill the void. What does that void feel like? What does it feel to have my soul occupy emptiness? It's serene, quiet, and not another sound can be heard. It is deep, endless it seems. Its darkness has a richness, a density to it that makes it feel solid and that can be reached out and touched, but my hands don't feel any feedback. Although it is empty, there is an ominous feeling of something watching over me, something embedded in this darkness. It feels like something is just beyond my sight. Those two ideas of emptiness and of the hovering feeling of being watched are blended together here. The ominous, threatening feeling forces me to move and react to fear. I don't want to, but there is no other option. There is no place to go, but I pace quicker,

178 Past the Horizon

only for those steps to turn into leaps and bounds. I realize that I am running, running from something that may or may not be there. And the faster I run, the closer it seems to be. In the span of a few minutes, it feels like I've occupied this space for hours, even days, running. The fear continually building until I try to scream. A scream that feels like I witnessed the greatest horror committed right in front of me, a scream of pure panic. I feel the exertion in my lungs and throat, but not a sound can be heard. The density of that darkness swallows any sound before it could reach past its domain. I hear nothing, see nothing, and feel nothing.

I slowly stop to catch my breath. As I go down on hand and knee, breathing heavy, I recognize, in addition to this ominous feeling, there is a constant pressure. That pressure surrounds me, slowly building, and it pulls me to even farther depths in this abyss, sinking me past the ground. I resist at first, but eventually have to give in to this. And as I am falling into even farther depths, I notice I am fully submerged in this fear, filled in a pool of it. It eventually seeps into my pores and begins to infect my veins, feeling it spread with every pulse of this broken heart.

That pressure slowly decreases and that fear vanishes. All the fears, anxieties, insecurities, even bodily pains are all cast aside, like dead branches. Out of this nothingness, a small spark is ignited in my soul. That spark feeds on all of those fears, anxieties, and desires. It grows bigger past the point of control. It's fury, its rage, it engulfs me. That urge to kill courses through my veins. To kill or be killed, it doesn't matter to me which outcome happens. I have lost my reason to even live. The adrenaline gives me a high, making me feel no more pain, only rage. There is nothing else that can be done with this raging flame. It can be directed at best, but needs to be burned out naturally. It is too big to try and quell. Its flames encompass all memories and thoughts, and it gets to the point of even eating away some of my sanity.

The flames start to slowly subside. They almost engulfed my entire being. And yet I do nothing about it. I am willing to accept the consequences as its power is a drug that I crave. That flame leaves pieces of my soul in ashes. The flame, built from rage such vigor coursing through my veins. After that rush slowly dies down and that adrenaline leaves my veins, I find myself in a void again. But this one feels different. It feels like everybody is watching me, even though not even a single soul can be found. I see a reflection posed in front of me. I see the image but cannot recognize him. The image I see in front of me is a man who is battered, bruised, scarred. There seems to be no life in his eyes. It seems like it is existing in a state not so different to dead. That reflection stares back, also confused. It took me one too many moments to realize who it was that I was seeing, my heart. I see now just how much pain and misuse it has had to endure. It breaks me, just like at the beach. Shame immediately engulfs me. That shame provided an avenue for all those cast away fears and anxieties to come back. They leave me feeling weak as those feelings penetrate deeper and with no route to escape this place. I drop to my knees and cradle myself in a fetal position, broken and no will to stand up with the only thing I want to do is soak in these feelings.

My heart watches this unfold, and the second that I lie on the floor it realizes who it is staring at. It tries to reach out to pull me up off of my knees, but all the effort is in vain. It tries to reconnect with me to feel whole again, but no matter how hard it tries it's always a bit too short, so close. It finally recoils its hands and starts to walk away. I don't even notice that my heart is leaving me until it is too late to call it back. The reality of my situation comes to fruition. I am alone, truly alone, I have nothing to protect anymore. Not even my own heart cares to be here. The weight of guilt impairs my movements: first from the sacrifice of myself to fuel my rage, second from allowing my heart to leave. So I sit in the null, in the nothingness, and slowly this space vanishes. It spits me back into reality.

I get up, now with the pressure of that void lifted off of my shoulders. I pick up the remnants of my soul in an effort to piece it back together, but it's incomplete. Every image feels dulled, and my physical limits have suddenly dropped to only be able to move one step. The anxiety creeps in, similar to at the beach, but this time as a raging tidal wave, making me feel that reminiscent tingling everywhere and forcing me to fidget. The depression settles after and builds in my mind. It begins the self-doubt and the phrase of "never good enough" reappears over and over again. Every time it is reiterated, it feels like that same dagger being slowly pushed into my heart deeper and deeper. And then I look up in the empty ceiling, as I lay there still and ask, "What did I do God?" The silence grows again, and I grow tired of it. "So many times I have asked you for something, anything, even a single word, and you leave me with silence, just like she has. Am I not worthy of the effort to you, either? Fine, I'll do this my way. I'll prove to you that I am worth more than this miserable place."

I stand with my aching legs, with shin splints running through my calves and knees stiff from the lack of fluids. I stand with my head held down from my shoulders stuck in a hunched position, and my arms feel feeble. I stand, and now I begin to walk. That tree, the one I carried in my dream, I feel its weight on my shoulders again, but I now see its potential. I will make this failure the very thing that will propel my climb to the heavens and through the seas. I will do so in defiance of God and the fate he put me in, and maybe she will finally see the potential I carry in myself. And I carry this weight, the tree that marks my failure, again.

The first few steps to get out of bed are fueled by only one thing, revenge. Each step I take is a touch faster and with force to try and hurt the ground with each step. My breaths are as if I am trying to steal all the oxygen out of the air. My gaze is piercing and able to gaze through a person's façade and into their soul and pull out of them their true intentions. I walk, and as I walk, I gain a total ruggedness, I form my soul into a serrated blade one that has withstood many blows willingly, but now with the taste for fighting back. I walk alone, formally from the feelings of shame and guilt for housing this void in my heart and soul. I have felt shame for pushing people away and for realizing I have become less human from this. Now I walk alone to mend my soul once again. With each step it begins to fill the piece that was lost in that fury. It is hollow and has no substance right now, but it will be enough to continue to move forward. I choose the path of the desperado to save my soul, or what remains of it. *"Walk. We must walk this path alone. There is nobody in our way anymore. We will carve this path with our own two feet and two hands if we have to. We will not die here. We will meet God at his gates and show him we made it there with our own two hands."*

How did I get here? How did I fall so low when I feel freedom's doors right in front of me? How did I get here back to being chained, this time by the very thing I tried to nurture and grow? How did my soul break again? Was it her? Was it because I put my faith in her? What was it? There have been many people in my life, some permanent, but most temporary. There have been some that have defined me as a friend, and others as an enemy, but most paid no attention to me. And out of all them, she was the only one to spark my spirit, the only one to make me forget of the lighthouse, as I saw her spirit shine brighter than the full moon on a dark night and the sun on a clear day. I saw her presence more calming than the soothing waves of the ocean. I saw the tenacity in her eyes, and it fed the fire in my soul. I was so close to happiness. Was I not content with where I was before I met her? Was it not good enough to just be happy by myself for a moment? Why wasn't it enough?

Connection

THE DAYS AFTER MY RESIGNATION, I feel freer than I have ever felt. My mind is clear and my body well rested. Colors feel more vibrant and smells more potent. It is such a unique experience that it takes me a few days to recognize this as peace, far from where I am now. I feel steady, with no mood swings or perspective shifts. Nothing I hear can waver my mental stability and balance. I am alone for most if not all of the day. Although it is a bit monotonous, I feel ok with it for the first time. There are a few days that I revel in this nothingness so that I can recollect myself for a moment and catch my breath.

But then the yearning to do something comes back. The thought of me wasting time sitting around builds in my mind. It prompts me to want to move, to do something, to start a project, to workout, to do something other than lie down and rest. It feeds on the insecurity of, "What if I didn't do enough? What if there's more to do? What if…?" I've felt this too many times, though. I've been at this crossroads hundreds, if not thousands, of times in my life, and almost every time I look back at these dilemmas, I've made the wrong choice. I've rushed it. My mind will always find things to do, I've come to realize, but in trying to do so much I have lost touch with the basics, the fundamentals. And so instead of the typical response to that question, I pose a series of questions to myself, "How many meals did I eat today? How much water did I drink? How much sleep did I get last night?" If the answers to those questions are sufficient for me, then I will consider engaging in a new project. But I know the answers the second I pose the questions. They aren't ideal. The habits I formed the last few years need to be remolded or else I will be put back into the same position regardless of what direction I take.

I use those questions as my daily reminders, to ensure this new self will remain longer than the last one, hopefully until the end of my days. I need a few habits to work on, so I choose the most basic: to sleep eight hours a night, to drink three liters of water, to eat three meals a day, and train at least once a day no matter how hard or light. They are basic, but if I can't uphold them then how would I ever be able to uphold this reformed self? How would I ever be able to cross that ocean? How would I ever be able to reach the lighthouse? So every day, with the diligence of a blacksmith forming his sword, of a monk reciting his daily prayers, I work on these habits. For weeks, this is all I cared for, to make sure these habits are engrained in me to the point of it being second nature. It takes me all that time to feel normalized again, for my body to recover from the long days, the short nights, and the grueling hours. My mind re-adjusts from all the negative cycles, all the self-doubt, all the insecurities. Even at the gym, where it's more acceptable to fall into savagery, I do not entertain it. I want to make the distinction that I am there for the love of challenging myself, not for the indulgence of my inner fury. It is new to me, to not unlock Pandora's box. But I know that if I dive into that realm that housed my insecurities for fuel that it will pull me in again, forcing me back to those vicious cycles. My heart requires me to conquer these feelings and the progress of the day-to-day fundamentals helped, but I still hold onto them. I don't know how to engage in doing so, for regularly feeling something other than pride is a new sensation for me. For as the days pass, I feel joy for life again.

Balance feels like it is near, and my internal foundation is in the process of settling. I feel as if I am knocking on destiny's doors, just waiting patiently for the tides to settle to allow myself to ship out to the horizon. The habits I am forming are beginning to become second nature as I have intended. "One more day" is the mantra I start with every morning, to make sure I stay committed to these tasks. Life feels simple, and I am content, but then God presents me with something my heart has been calling out for, love.

One morning, I get a random notification from my phone. It is from the app I downloaded weeks prior. I get a message from a woman who liked my profile. I am curious, so I decide to open it. My eyes witness a picture of a beautiful woman. She has blue-eyes, full lips, and a soft, round nose. Her hair is dark brown that stopped around her mid-back. She has a fair skin, a shade or two darker than being full-fledged white. I can tell she is Latina. She has a slim figure and is dressed conservatively in all of her photos.

I feel excitement in my stomach, for it feels like the first new stimulus in my life in a long time. Before I respond to her, I ask myself, "Am I ready to try again?" It is a question for my heart alone, for it has been waiting in the background diligently. It calls out, "Yes." It builds up anticipation in my hands to open up the phone and message her back. But I reclaim myself for a moment to ask myself one more question, "Has the foundation settled? Am I ready to build on top of it?" "Almost, just give me a bit more time." My heart doesn't care. It sees the opportunity for what it wants and it takes the steering wheel. "I'm sure I'll be ready. I'm sure it will be fine." It is false confidence, just something I say to encourage myself to take this opportunity and I don't want to waste it.

"Hi, I'm…"

"Hey, how are you?" I don't know what to say. I am so excited that my mind goes with what feels natural, so I decide to just treat it like a normal conversation between friends.

Luckily, she responds. "I'm good. What about you?"

"Doing good. Just enjoying the free time on my hands. Have some time between jobs."

"Oh nice. What have you been doing to fill your free time?"

"Just been relaxing. Working on a few things, but nothing exciting."

The conversation progresses naturally, as we both seem interested enough to stay engaged. I want to talk about everything I have been doing since then, but I stay reserved for now. So instead of going that route in the conversation, I ask her what led her here.

She responds, "Well, there's been a lot I've had to deal with, and I don't know I kind of just tried this as a last effort. Didn't really expect much from this."

"Well, here we are. We might as well enjoy it. I'm open to seeing where this takes us."

"Yeah, me too. What about you? What brought you here?"

"I don't want to repeat what you said, but I felt as though I need something else to continue on my journey and maybe, just maybe it's somebody instead of something."

"I like that."

From then on, the conversations grows more and more. We become much more open to each other, and for the first time in my life, I want to be completely open with another person. Up to this point, we've only shared words through the phone, but they seem to be the most genuine words I have shared with another, and I am sure she feels the same sentiment.

Time passes much quicker with her words comforting my heart every day. I soon forget about the mantra I have told myself to recite every day, "One more day, one more meal, one more glass of water." That mantra will soon get replaced with, "I hope she sent me a message before bed." For the time being, I keep the routine of eating and drinking and training every day. Those habits have taken a foothold and have formed fully. I find pride in regaining the sustenance my body needs and feel like the diligence I have to work on those habits pays off. And I get the added benefit of seeing my heart full of hope, hope for something that I believe to have been lost to me.

It has been weeks since me and ___ have been talking, and the excitement in meeting her grows more and more. She tells me about her path to her dream, and she seems so committed to it that it my admiration for her grows. She went back to school and has an end goal in sight, one that would remain a mystery to me for a while. We talk about hobbies we liked doing, and she is also into running and lifting, and it helps entice my thoughts of her more, as I think of doing those things with her. My love for her grows every time I think about her.

So I finally muster up the courage to ask, "Hey, so what are you doing Saturday?"

"I'm busy in the morning, but I'm free the rest of the day. What's up?"

"What would you say if I asked for some company for a midday coffee date?"

"Depends, who would you like to accompany you?"

I can tell she is joking, but I like her quick-witted response.

"You, of course."

"Well, then I'd say I'd love to go."

"Well then, sounds like your schedule just got a bit busier that day."

"Yeah, I guess it has."

That Saturday could not have come any sooner. The quickness of how the days go suddenly halts and soon feels like each day drags on. But it gives me some time to refocus on those basics. I feel like the energy I spend talking to her, although serene, distracts me from the big picture. Every word she shares with me entices me to draw closer to her, and it moves my focus away from the lighthouse. So I regain a bit of composure and stick with the basics again, not to say I wasn't before, but I lost the intention in doing those actions. I don't want to slip again, not to that baseless being, so that fear keeps me in line for a bit longer.

Friday night finally arrives, and I feel the butterflies in my stomach. I want to get a good night's rest but those emotions make it difficult. "Tomorrow, I finally get to meet her." Reciting those words still fills me with that same feeling even today. But I try my best to find some foothold of calmness, so I hold on to it and anchor my mind so that it can settle down and rest.

Finally, the day is here. I can meet the woman who has filled me with hope these last few weeks. I take a longer shower than usual and scrub my body a touch harder to ensure I clean myself as best as possible. I had already picked my outfit out the night before. I am that excited for this. I check my phone and see if she messaged me since. Our conversations have become day-long events, and we end them with "good nights" and start them with "good mornings." The same is true for that day.

I message her as the clock approaches the time we were supposed to meet, "Hey, so I'll be heading out soon. I'll be there in about thirty minutes."

"Ok, I'm caught up with something, so I'll be a bit late, but I'll see you there."

I don't think much of it, so I decide to leave about fifteen minutes later than what I said. I get there and let her know a few minutes later.

"Hey, just got here. Take your time, though. I'll just be walking around for a bit."

"Ok, I'll let you know when I'm on the way. Sorry, still catching up with something."

"No worries."

Time passes so slowly, and as each minute passes I begin to wonder, "Will she even show?" I sit in my truck as the clock continues to run. Twenty minutes pass, nothing. Many old memories of reminiscent scenarios play in my head. I don't want this to turn out the same, so I decide to stick it out a bit longer. Forty minutes pass, and I ask, "Hey is everything ok?"

I get a response about ten minutes later, "Yeah, I'm sorry. I'll be heading over in a bit. Just been busy with stuff at the house."

"Oh ok. Do you want me to order you something?"

"No, that's ok."

"Ok, I'll see you soon."

My mind was already shut off, and I started to feel a bit bitter. It was a natural response, for I felt like I have been here before, at a spot waiting for some woman, or not even getting a response back. That left a sour taste in my mouth. I wait another twenty minutes or so, and finally I see a car pull up. Instantly, the disdain in my heart dissipates and is replaced by a nervousness. She drives a nice Subaru, and I am a bit impressed. She steps out, and the same woman I saw in the photos appears. I am a bit speechless, and frankly intimidated. She wears a grey zip-up sweater and under it a red tank top. She has on some jeans and some nice Jordans on. She makes a simple outfit look stunning.

"Hey, sorry I'm late."

"Oh no that's ok. I didn't have much planned today anyways."

"How are you? Did you already get your order?"

"Yeah, I got it. Want me to get you something?"

"Oh no, that's ok. I'll just go grab something in there real fast, and we can talk outside. It's nice out."

"Yeah, it is."

As I get my seat outside, those feelings come back, the ones of a resentful kid and my mind begins to close. I can't shake the fact that she is this late with not that good of an explanation. As she comes out with her drink, we discuss things we said on texts, but I can tell I am being standoffish. I try my hardest to fight off those old memories, but they feel too strong, and so I shut myself off. The intimidation of seeing such a beautiful woman also makes words hard for me to say, so I try to keep responses short but genuine. I am a nervous wreck, fighting off old thoughts, and I know she can tell, too.

The date goes by with seemingly nothing meaningful coming out of it besides me being too timid to say anything. I didn't want to make a wrong step, so I reverted to not making any. The date lasted about an hour, and it felt awkward from start to finish. We ended up hugging and decided to leave right after. I knew I blew it.

A few weeks pass with less contact between us. We text, but nothing of substance ever seems to come up. It is only the casual responses like,

"How are you?"

"Good and you?"

"Good. What's new?"

"Nothing much."

That seems to be the extent of a lot of our conversations for a few weeks. The rest of summer passes, and we slowly become only friends with no more intention besides saying hi every once and a while when we're bored. That seems to be where destiny placed us. During that time, I don't focus on much else. I don't care to try and meet somebody else. Even though a few more notifications come from that app, I only entertain the conversations to see if they merit any more time or energy. They don't spark my mind as much as she had. The thought of her stays in the back of my mind, and the question "What if?" pops up in my head.

As the days continue to pass, our messages become more infrequent to the point where we stop talking entirely. I don't like it as it feels like I've witnessed the same story being played over again. And as she leaves, so with it that hope. It deflates me a bit, enough to not try and look for somebody else. So I go back to the basics, back to the shadows for a few more weeks, back to forming these habits I have lost focus on. I give myself until my birthday in a month, hoping that these habits will be finally cured by then.

My birthday, a day of reckoning, one where my past mistakes find a way to judge me. Each year that passes, it seems more and more difficult to get through that day. For many years, I have tried to salvage it, to try and create new memories instead of being captive to old ones. That day is the only day of the year where I want to give in, to quit, to just be at home by myself looking at that empty ceiling. I tried to break this habit in recent years. I tried to inject good memories, but they all seemed to backfire, only digging deeper into the wounds of my heart. As I approach this day, the flashbacks come back, especially of the recent years. My mind presents them all to me in a way where they are meshed together as time slowly molds them into one general feeling of resentment, instead of unique thoughts and feelings. But I still engage in trying to comb through the chaos, even though I know it is a malicious cycle, one I have yet to part with.

Ten years old, I gave up on this day back then. Why? I don't even know. I just felt an uneasiness to that day back then. Was it a naïve kid hoping to look cool as he shrouded himself in mystery? Was it a kid who didn't want the disappointment of another failed birthday party, one filled with strangers instead of friends? Was it a kid who felt the grip of depression take hold of him? I think it was all the above. Many of those younger birthdays were not much of note. I just kept my head down, hoping nobody would say happy birthday in class. But there always seemed to be one teacher who would bring it up. I didn't care for presents, or money, I barely even wanted cake. The sweet tooth in me was the only thing that was happy each year as I knew I would get a nice chocolate cake to myself. As I grew and left the house, that was when the sting of that day worsened.

The first birthday away from home felt the loneliest, but I felt no pain, only void. I had not experienced enough life to merit the feeling of pain. I was at the apartment I was renting at the time. It was a small two-bedroom apartment, with old hardwood floors that creaked with every step I took. The walls were an old knockdown white that had excessive layers of paint that almost made them look purely smooth. My room was about twelve feet by twelve feet at the most and had just enough room for a dresser and the full-size bed that I had taken from home. It was simple, only there for one purpose, to give me a roof over my head to sleep. I told my parents that I didn't want to do anything for that day, which was routine, and they obliged. I was at college most of the day anyways, and thankfully it distracted me enough to get through it relatively unscathed. The loneliness was heavier when I got home, for I had no other distractions to use to hide from this feeling. That loneliness triggered tears to fall down my face. At the time, I didn't understand why I didn't feel sadness or pain physically, but now I realize that it was the vain attempts of my heart to show its grief. My ears were deaf to its calls.

A few years passed like this, with no highs and no lows, as nothingness filled my birthday. And as they did, I too became closer to nothing. I moved apartments and was in a spot that had a bit more room. School was still the main focal point in my life, but I knew that I needed some company. My confidence was low—lower than now even—and I found it difficult to talk to any girls during school. So instead, I got a dog, a chow-husky mix named Lucy. She had golden amber fur, and the cutest face for a dog. Nobody could convince me otherwise. She had a bit of a temper issue with other dogs, but she loved humans. She was my first real dog, The family had one when I was younger, but it was more my parents' dog than mine or my siblings'. I cared for this dog more than any other thing in this world at that time. I would wake up early, before work and school to take her to the park that was a fifteen- minute walk. It would be down to fifteen degrees outside, but I still took her. She was a mix of two breeds that loved the cold, and I felt it would be an injustice to not take her to enjoy it. I would come home between class breaks to walk her again, even if it was for only fifteen minutes. When I got home, I would walk her a normal two- to three-mile route around downtown. And again, whether rain, snow, sunshine, or clouds, I would take her. There were times that I dressed up in four layers to make sure she could enjoy the snow. She was happy, I could see it in her eyes, and that made me happy, even if it was only superficial. Her time with me was short as she had cancer, and it was rapidly accelerating. It shocked me, but I stayed composed till her last days even though I saw her health rapidly decline almost every day. I had to put her down a week before my birthday. That was the first dose of pain that was attached to my birthday. It gripped me, as it was the catalyst the void needed to pull me in, but it helped me cope with the idea of death and how close it can truly be.

The year after that, I was out of school and finally started my professional career. When I finally realized how bland I was, I tried new hobbies. I was invited to a Latin dancing event and decided to go but only as a favor for a friend. It was a bit nerve-racking at the beginning, but I overcame that. I learned to not care about what people thought of me. When I was out there, I only listened to the music and let it move my feet. After some time going to these socials, I ended up meeting a woman. She seemed very reserved as I would see her around the same events I would go to. We even danced a few times, but she never seemed interested in me. It was a shock when she asked for my number. Things between us moved fast, and I felt like everything I said seemed to make her smile. We enjoyed our company, and I wanted to try and rewrite the bad memory I had the previous year for my birthday. So I asked her if she would teach me about camping as I never got into it and I wanted to give it a shot. She obliged and we chose the weekend of my birthday. Tensions began to climb that week as we were preparing for the trip, and they seemed to spill over the day we left for the camp spot. We took her car as she offered to pick me up. On the drive, we said nothing to each other, as I felt like saying anything would light a fire I did not want to put out. She also said nothing. We both knew something was off.

We got to the camp spot and every word I said seemed to pop off an argument. I wish I had kept my mouth shut. The day drew to a close.

As we sat by the fire, as she said, "This isn't going to work out anymore."

I knew those words to be true, but I didn't want to accept them. But I responded in kind, "So you think this is the end?"

"Yeah."

It left me so confused, and I found myself asking questions I shouldn't have. "Was I not good enough? Did she find another person? Why now, on my birthday? Does she hate me? What did I do wrong?"

We had to stay the night as she was the one who drove, and I didn't have anybody to come and pick me up, she called the shots. I had to share a tent with a woman who I believed to have loved me at one point but now felt nothing. I didn't sleep at all. We left the morning after, and she dropped me off. What I believed to have been loneliness a few years ago was merely only a sample. What I felt that day was deeper. Not a single call from anybody all weekend. I tried calling everybody on my phone, except her, and I got nothing but voicemail every time. That was the day I realized that I could not rely on anybody else to save me from those feelings. So my options were to conquer this void myself or revel in it. I chose the latter even though I believed to have followed the former. That day replays in my mind. Could I have said something before to prolong that separation? Could I have ended things earlier? None of it mattered now but those questions still hover.

The year after, my aunt (my mom's sister) and uncle (my dad's brother) died right around the same time of year. I felt a distant sadness, as I knew they were family, but it did not hit me as hard as my parents did. What really hit me was the idea that my birthday was slowly becoming a catalyst for more events like this. It made me not want to even acknowledge that day anymore. The stories seemed to pile up year after year, and I did not want to fall into that trap again.

This year, with the reformation of many habits and ideals, I want to offer this day one final act of solace. I want to do nothing but for the last time. And I even commit to telling a few close friends that my birthday was coming up. My friend from Sacramento, and a few judo people, those are the only people I decide to tell. I don't really have expectations, but a simple text of acknowledgement would be more than enough.

So the day comes, I sit on my bed and just stare at that ceiling. Hours pass and my phone is silent, not a single notification pops up all day. I wonder, "Did I not text people that today was my birthday?" So I scroll through my text messages to ensure that I did, which is true. As I scroll, I see the text messages between me and that woman from the app. I decide to read some of the older conversations we shared, and soon she is the only thought in my head. She is the only person I have been able to think about that didn't bring up past memories and even distracts my mind from the fact that the few people I called good friends all forgot my birthday. My heart again yearns for her. We only had one date, and it went poorly, but still, my heart wants her. So I go to bed and sleep on it to see if that sentiment is still there the day after. It is. In response to that, I pick up the phone and message her again.

"Hey, long time."

"Yeah, it has. How are you?"

"I'm doing all right..."

The conversations flow again like the first time we talked. I didn't know what I wanted from her, whether it was merely to be friends, to be something more, or to try and reach new heights and share the rest of my days with her. As we began to discuss things again, that very topic came up,

"What made you talk to me again?"

"Honestly, I've been thinking about that date and know that I didn't do myself justice. I'm sorry if I came across kind of closed off."

"Yeah, you were definitely an asshole. But I still enjoyed what we talked about before the date. I see a lot of potential in you."

"Honestly, I feel the same way. I don't know where the road will take us, but I'm willing to find out."

"I think I like that idea."

We start our relationship as friends but as the time grows, so does our connection. The messages slowly evolve to calls on the phone that last for hours, and even after we continue messaging. I eventually become more confident, and we have a second date.

We decide on having a late lunch date downtown and walking along the river that passes through the middle of the city. There's a nice trail that doesn't take long and has a great view of the river and the Sierra Mountains. I take her hand and I lead the way. A few minutes pass just admiring the scenery, mainly her, but the trees were nice, too, I guess.

I ask, "So I don't think I ever asked you, but what do you want to do with your life?"

"I want to go to school to be an engineer."

"Really? No way. You won't believe this."

"What?"

"I'm an engineer."

"If you can make it, then I have a good chance. Hehe."

"Quite the witty one, aren't you?"

"Yes, yes, I am. Haha. You should have noticed by now."

"Sorry, I'm usually distracted by your beauty."

I notice her turn to hide her blushing cheeks. I'm so focused on her that it was impossible to miss. I continue and ask, "What made you choose engineering?"

"Well, I have this weird dream. It will take a long time to explain but a part of it is to help build structures and buildings in low resource areas, and I need the engineering certificates to do that."

"How long have you had this idea in mind? I'm not afraid to listen. I can make enough time to sit down and hear it."

"Ever since I was a kid, I knew I wanted to be an engineer. I've wanted to help people and I think I found a way to do both."

"Wow."

"What?"

"I'm just amazed."

"You're pretty amazing, too."

"Why do you say that?"

"You just seem so confident in yourself. Like you know where you want to go. You might not know the final destination but you're willing to take the climb to find out."

"Honestly, it's taken a lot to get here. I never would have considered myself confident, even up 'til now. Thank you."

"You don't need to thank me. I'm just recognizing a good soul."

She turns the tables on me and forces me to hide my blush. I hold her hand a bit tighter as we walk. Time seems to just flow as fast as the words do between us. As we get to the end of the trail, we see the sun about to resign for the day. The mountain silhouettes glow with a vivid red and blocks the sun so that we have the chance to appreciate the beautiful colors unfold in front of us. I take her other hand so we can look at each other. I lock on her eyes through her glasses. *So soft, so innocent, so...perfect,* I think. I get nervous but I don't let them get to me before I have a chance to seal this moment with a kiss. I lean forward, hoping, praying that she meets me with her lips, and she does. Her soft lips seem to encapsulate mine and fill my heart with something I have never felt before. It was just a simple kiss, but I know from that point on that she has me.

"I've grown to admire you more. The more you tell me, the more I realize how unique your soul is. It's a soul that houses a tenacity for your dream. After all this world has done to you. After all the pain you had to take on, you still want to build hope to those in need. It's amazing. It makes me want to chase my own dream, one that has evaded me for all this time."

"You will, and no matter how this ends, I want to be there to help you find it."

Those simple words fill me with so much energy. The word that tries to encapsulate this feeling is love, but it doesn't do it justice. It feel like my soul finally found a counterpart that burns with a similar fury, and our flames dance around each other as our sign to the heavens to see our souls begin to merge. It feels like my mind found a contemporary, one to bounce ideas off of and find unique ways to handle any challenge with. It feels like my heart is beating at the same rate hers is at all times of the day, like we are in sync in more ways than just mentally or spiritually. That feeling, that connection, so genuine, so pure, so unique. I know, and still believe, that I could not feel anything like this with any other woman.

"Is this truly what love feels like? If so, whatever the price for this, I'll pay it. I'll pay it a thousand times over to make sure we can feel this for the rest of our days. And when our time in this world is up, we will offer up our bodies so that our souls have the rest of eternity to experience this."

A few more months pass and we have spent many hours on the phone, fewer in person, but they are all memorable. We try to find some time to see each other throughout the day. The most consistent times we can see each other are on her lunch break, or right before she starts her night shifts. I remember the first time ever bringing her food for her lunch and seeing her a bit surprised.

"Hey, stranger."

"Hey, what are you doing here?"

"Oh, just wanted to drop something off. I got you some Wendy's for your lunch. Sorry if it's not anything special. I know you deserve a nicer meal. It was kind of a last-minute idea."

I saw her smile just a little bit, almost innocently.

She responds, "Thank you. You didn't have to."

"I know. But I did anyways. Just trying to make your night a bit easier."

"You did. I actually forgot to bring food today. Hehe."

"Well, looks like my timing is impeccable. Hehe. Have a great night at work, ok?"

"I will now. Thank you again."

"Anything for you."

We share a long hug and a few kisses before she goes in to work. Ever since that day, I want to see that smile on her face all the time. So I keep buying her meals for lunch just for the excuse to see her, and sometimes coffee in the morning. It isn't much time that we see each other, but I treasure every second. Every time she leaves makes me yearn for her more and more. In response to that I ask her something.

"What are you doing next Friday?"

"I don't think I have much. What do you have going on?"

"Nothing, I was actually thinking of taking you out to dinner. As much as I like spending dinner at your work's parking lot, I think we should try something new. And I know neither of us dress up much, and I figured it would be nice to go out and dress fancy for a night."

"I like that idea. Do you have reservations set up?"

"Yeah, for seven PM at the Grille. You know that place right by the riverside?"

"Oh yeah. Never been. But it sounds like a good place."

"Yeah, I've heard good things about it. Let's go?"

"Of course. I'm looking forward to it. I think I have an outfit already picked out in my head."

"Oh yeah? What are you going to wear?"

"I can't tell you. It's a surprise."

"Damn, you're going to make me wait, huh?"

"Yep."

She has already taken my heart, and I know that night will be special. Any moment with her is special. I will still get nervous seeing her, even if it's only for a few minutes in passing. But when we start talking, the words will flow out of me effortlessly and my soul would feel at home. There was no feeling of void as her presence filled it and overflowed my heart with emotions.

The day comes closer than I thought. I get ready, wearing a nice fitted polo, some slim fit slacks, and some nice brown dress shoes that I polished for thirty minutes the night before. I want to look nice for her.

She meets me at my house as she lives a bit more north than I do, and she wanted to meet me here. I'm dressed waiting in my living room as impatient as a child waiting for his candy after Halloween. After those tortuous minutes pass, I finally hear the doorbell ring. I check the peephole, and it's her. I open it and witness the greatest beauty I have seen.

"Hey, you look…stunning. You almost got me speechless."

"Hey, handsome, you clean up nice yourself."

I instantly notice that she put on makeup, mascara, and eye-liner along with a bit of blush to cover her cheeks. She has some neutral-colored lipstick that makes her lips all that more enticing to kiss. She sports a black-laced top, showing her curves more than she usually does. She matches it with a nice suit that presents the silhouette of her body well. She has on heels, something that is new to see, and she seems a bit uncomfortable in them. It is a bit chilly outside, so she is wearing a red sweater, which does not go with the rest of her outfit, but she is still able to pull it off. I'm convinced nobody else could.

While seated at dinner, it is hard not to take my eyes off her.

"What are you looking at?"

"Oh…uh…nothing. I just…I just think you look beautiful."

She turns away as I see her blush and try to hide a smile. She doesn't respond, and she doesn't need to. Her reaction shows what she wants to say.

I continue, "You wanna know something?"

"Yeah, sure."

"I don't know what it is, but I'm glad I went and talked to you again. I'm glad you're in my life right now. I can't really describe it, but when I'm with you I've grown comfortable with you, like I don't have any pressure over my shoulders."

"That's ironic."

"What?"

"I was thinking the same thing. I look in your eyes and know I'm ok. I've grown to love when I'm in your arms. It makes me feel safe. I don't think about anything else."

The tables quickly turn, and I find myself being the one to hide my red cheeks and to turn away.

"I hope we can make this last for a long time."

"Me too."

The food arrives shortly after, and the waiter asks, "Is there anything else you two need?"

I look over at my date and respond to the waiter, "No, I have everything I need right in front of me."

Another small smile forms on her face as she tries to hide it from the waiter.

"Sound's good. Enjoy the food."

"Thank you."

As we finish our food, I ask, "Well, what do you want to do now?"

"I think it's time for some dessert?"

"Ooh, I love sweets. I'm in."

"I know you do. Let's go to this ice cream spot not too far from here."

"Ok, want to walk or should we drive?"

"It's too cold outside. I'm not walking."

"Ok, I'll grab the truck."

A smile fills my face as I head to the truck. I feel such a high, and it is not even over. We head over to this small ice cream shop, and I binge on a few large scoops of some homemade ice cream. She ate a bit as well. We both are fat kids at heart, and it shows that night.

"Oh, party foul!" she says.

"What? What happened?"

"You got some ice cream on your shirt. Hahaha!"

"Oh, my bad. Hahaha. I can't eat ice cream slow. It's too good...Look at your shirt though."

She looks down and she notices an ice cream stain on her sweater that matches mine. We both laugh even louder.

I comment, "Dude, I'm so full. But this stuff is too good not to finish."

"Yeah, I know, I can barely finish mine."

"Momma told me to never waste food. So if you can't finish, I guess I'll have to take one for the team and eat the leftovers. Hehe."

"Well, she raised a good man it seems. I think I'm stuffed. Have the rest of mine."

"I mean, if I have to. Hehe."

As we end our detour to the ice cream shop, we head back to my house. She holds my hand as we drive back and caresses my arm tightly with hers. She is resting a bit from the food coma. She looks so innocent in my arms. I feel like I saw a glimpse of heaven that night, like God gave me the task to accompany an angel. We get home, and I believe the night will end right there. She surprises me with what she tells me next.

"I was actually thinking of just staying the night with you, if that's ok."

It is more than ok with me. It is a blessing. "Of course, you can."

We stay downstairs for a moment as I play a few slow dance bachata songs. We both enjoy that style of music, and I have some experience dancing it, so I want to teach her the basics. I take her hand, and we get close, with no space between our bodies.

As the song fills the room, we lock eyes. I cannot hold those words anymore, so I decide to cave and say, "I love you."

Without hesitation, she responds, "I love you, too."

We share a kiss, one that interlocks our souls, and I know that I want to do anything and everything with this woman. I never knew those few words would fill my heart with such vigor, such vitality. For the first time in a long time, I pray to God that this moment will never end.

We go upstairs shortly after and prepare for bed. She takes out her contacts while she is in the bathroom. As she walks out, I see her with her natural eye color for the first time, a dark brown, almost black. So dark, it could look into one's soul. I allow her eyes to examine mine. She looks at me with such vulnerability, as if to say, "Take me, for I am yours and you are mine." So I caress her close, and we kiss. The kiss naturally evolves to us stripping bare. We share the bed, not as two separate beings, but of one with two separate bodies. I feel the radiance of her skin caress my own body as we lie next to each other. She is vulnerable to me, and I to her. We trust each other completely with every scar on our bodies, every insecurity in our minds, every tear in our hearts. We give into each other completely. The passion of that night will forever live on in my soul and in hers. And from that moment, a thought grows in my head. *I want this woman to be in my life for the rest of my days. No matter what I have to do, I will.*

We lay together the rest of the night, and I wake up more rejuvenated than ever before because my heart has finally been given the sustenance it craves. I see her asleep, and it only grows that overwhelming revelation in my head. "She is mine. God, how did you see me fit to caress an angel like this?"

She wakes up shortly after as I am still holding her in my arms. She has a peaceful smile on her face as she looks at me, and we share a kiss. We know that moment comes to a close, but we also have hope that it would not be the last. We make sure it doesn't. The conversations we have slowly evolve from our individual dreams to how we would spend the days together. But she still holds her own dream close to her heart, and that fire burns bright in her to see it through. I want more moments with her as I become more infatuated by her. I am ok with her being my everything. It makes me lose my focus on what took me this far, the lighthouse. I never even think about it as my heart feels gluttonous and wants more.

A few weeks pass since that blessed night, and she messages me something different.

"Hey, my period is late."

I am in shock, as my head races a bit thinking about the one thing that usually means.

"Are you telling me you're pregnant?"

"I don't know. I haven't tested yet, but I just wanted to let you know."

I know how I want to respond and what I am going to do, and I need to let her know, too.

"Hey, well listen, if you are or you're not, I'm going to stay right by your side the entire way. Because you have something that I can't live without."

"What is that?"

"My heart."

"I love you."

"I love you, too."

So I buy a test and ask her to come over and take it. During that time, I reflect on what outcome we would likely get. And honestly, I was ok with either one. I know I want to be with her for the rest of my days, and I want to start a family with her. It doesn't matter to me if it is sooner rather than later. She gets here and proceeds to take the test. I wait as I know this answer may change my course of history forever. There is a dulled stillness filling the room as time stops for the both of us while we wait for the results. A single leaf blowing past the window would have disturbed that silence. Finally, the results appear.

Negative.

I look at her as we share a similar expression. One of disappointment.

She tells me, "Honestly, I kind of wanted this to happen. I want to be the mother of your children."

My heart immediately pounds and leaps out of my chest as I express a similar feeling.

"I wanted it, too. I've wanted to be a father for a long time."

"We can still make it happen."

I am in a bit of disbelief for what she proposes. I want to, I do, but I want to make sure she does, too.

"Are you sure?"

"Yes."

I see the reassurance in her eyes, and I know she is telling the truth. So we head upstairs and try, this time with full intent of doing so. The passion is as intense as the first time.

After we finish, I laid my head on her stomach as she tells me, "You're going to be a great father."

I immediately start to cry. I cannot hold back those tears. I don't know where they come from, but those words of affirmation from the woman I love pull such an emotion out of me that force me to cry. Tears of joy are an understatement. She is my destiny. I am sure of it.

The coming days are grueling as we have to wait a few weeks to make sure the test is as accurate as possible. I don't want to wait, but she makes the time much more enjoyable. We come up with some names for our child: Xavier Israel for a boy and Selena Rosa for a girl. Those names fill my mind with so many ideas. I daydream of all the things I want to do with my child, too many to even name. We would toss around ideas of how we would want our wedding to be too. If we wanted to start a family, we needed to start there.

"Where would you want to get married?" I ask.

"Somewhere where there's water. Maybe in Bali. I've always loved that spot. I want to move there one day."

I immediately search for wedding locations online and find Tibumana Waterfall and send her a photo of the venue.

"What about having it here?"

"Oh my God that's beautiful."

"It's in Bali, too."

"I'd go right now if I could."

"One day we will. We have to do one here for all of our friends and family."

"Yeah. Oooh I have an idea."

"Let's hear it."

"I know you told me that you never went to prom. What if we did a normal wedding and rented out a high school auditorium for after. It could just be me and you, we don't need anybody else. We could dance our favorite song like we were at prom."

I instantly thought, *She remembered all the small details I told her, and she knew for some reason this one always stung a bit, to not go to prom, or have a date to a dance.* To me it feels like for once that dream would come true, the dream of a young shy kid who had no confidence. How far I've come.

"I love you. I want to make it happen."

"We will. I love you too."

To think of the life we would live together and all the adventures we would embark on together slowly becomes my favorite way to fill the empty days . While we are waiting, she still focuses on school; I have a job lined up and am merely waiting for the start date. She had to take a job working the graveyard shift as a medical assistant to help her pay for school while still trying to actually got to school during the day. It only cemented the image I have of her as the woman of my dreams. During my days off, I clean up old books and whatnot to possibly prepare for a mini-me on the way. And in doing so, I find an old memo dated for 2016, five years ago.

> *I want kids. I know I want a family. I want a daughter. Maybe I'll name her Ashley. No, that doesn't resonate with me. Maybe something more like Kyla, something unique. I guess it's too early to come up with names for a baby that you may or may not have. I can't even get a girlfriend. How am I going to get a kid? It feels as if every day this dream fades away. Every day that I walk alone that dream runs farther away from my grasp, like a butterfly you try to catch in the park. It's something I feel I can never touch but get so close to it.*
>
> *I know right now that this dream takes a backseat to my other goals. But when will it become my priority? There has to be a point in time where I need to fulfill my other needs. I understand that at this moment I am submerged in my current goals, to finish college, to find a good job, to make a name for myself. I always wanted to become somebody to remember, regardless of how they see me. Hell, even though the Joker was a villain, and everybody knows who he is. If it wasn't for him Batman wouldn't be who he is. I'll be the villain if I have to be, but I don't want to*

be. I just want to be recognized. I want to be able to look into the face of my family and be happy. I want to have somebody by my side who doesn't even need to understand my pain or struggles but wants to try.

I want somebody who won't shy away from the darkness of my mind, as I won't shy away from hers. It seems like that simple requirement is too much for some girls. But it's not the only requirement. I want a woman, not a girl, who has ambition. A woman who has her own dream and will put nothing ahead of it until it is achieved. I want a woman who is beautiful in her outer shell, but not for any other reason but to please herself. She stays beautiful to present her best self to the world every day. I want a woman, somebody not afraid to take what she deserves. A woman who understands her weaknesses and improves on those every day. A woman who is not afraid to speak her mind, or express her true feelings. I know that it's a selfish dream of mine. A dream that will probably never be realized. It's a wish I don't hope to achieve because I lost all hope. But no matter how hopeless I say I am, I still hold on to a speck of it, just to get through the days. I want a woman who struggles, or has had to struggle, for what she has, down to the socks she wears. A woman like that is worth almost more than my own dream.

Reading that makes it seems like God is giving me the intuition to know what I want in life. And now He has presented me with just that, a family of my own. I feel blessed and it gives me hope for the future that seems not so distant anymore. I feel like I am on cloud nine and nothing can bring me down. Soon I am going to start my family.

The time finally comes for us to try a new test, and I am more nervous this time, for I now know what was at stake. We take the test at my place again. The silence that was there the previous time is replaced by the noise of my fidgeting around the living room. I cannot wait any longer. She steps out of the bathroom and reveals the result, negative. It deflates us both again, but this time me more than her. I fed it hope, and it lets me down again. Because she still had her own dream to anchor her. I forwent mine for her and the possibility of raising a child.

"It's ok, babe. Maybe it's just not our time just yet," I say those words to give myself some reaffirmation rather than console her.

"I know. I'm just a bit sad."

"Me too, but I'm still here, and I always will be."

We end the day with a kiss and the now consistent I love yous. After she leaves, I ponder what just happened. To say it doesn't surprise me would be a lie. It does. It defeats me. I want that more than I want to breathe. I was so close to having what I feel is my destiny.

And so I ask God, "Why did you tempt me with this again?" I wait diligently for a response, and not a sound is heard. Again, I thought, again He leaves me unanswered. It hit me harder than it should have, as after this day I begin to be more cautious and more concerned for the woman I love.

She tells me one day, "Hey, I think I'm going to look for a second job."

"Really? Are you sure you can handle it? You seem to be spreading yourself too thin with your current job, and school."

"I mean, I know I can handle a second job. I've done it before."

"Yeah, but school is just going to get harder. I know when I went to school, I had to spend a lot more time in getting things done."

"Yeah, but that's you. I know I can handle it."

"But I just don't like the idea."

"Well, that's your problem. I need to do what I have to do get by and pay for school. I know my limits. I have to go. I'll talk to you later."

"Ok. I love you."

She hangs up before saying it back. A pit grows in my stomach. I feel like the foundation we built has been shaken. I am a bit lost because I don't see anything wrong. I just don't want to see her struggle anymore, or at least not any worse. I just want to let her know that I care. So I text her not too long after.

"Hey, I'm sorry about the phone call."

"It's fine."

"I just wanted to let you know that I care for you. I'm sorry if it wasn't what you wanted to hear."

"Like I said, its fine."

"Ok well, if there's anything you need, let me know."

"Ok, I have to go. I got homework to do."

"Ok."

After dozens of similar conversations, I feel like I was slipping. I never felt like I was on solid ground with her. I am lost. I don't know what she thinks of me anymore. "Am I an enemy? What did I do wrong? Am I…not good enough?" The days continue to pass, and the comfort she gives me feels a bit less comforting. I know this was because I had the old image of her still replaying in my head. I am stuck in a paradox it seems, and even she couldn't get me out, it forces us to drift away from each other a bit. The connection we had is still strong enough to hold us together for the time being. But life is known to throw chaos when it has the chance and it did exactly that.

It is three in the morning. I get a call from a random person, "Hey, I'm calling you because your brother is in the hospital. He got jumped downtown and is in the ER. I'm calling because you're his emergency contact."

The noise of my phone was what woke me up, but I couldn't get up in time to answer it. The voicemail pops up immediately after, and I listen to it. I usually don't listen to random number's voice message from the excessive spam callers, but this time I do. I don't have any time to think. I move purely on instinct. I put on some sweats, a sweater, take my car keys, basically jump downstairs, and head to the hospital. I call back that number thinking it's the nurse, but it's his girlfriend. She tells me which room he is in, and I get there as fast as I can. Panic fills my veins the closer I get to the hospital. I am speeding all the way down and try to stay alert for any cop cars to make sure I can make it there as fast as possible. Luckily, there aren't. I park and instantly run to the ER entrance and immediately ask for my brother. They tell me the way to his room, and I pace rapidly. I see his figure from a distance, and I know that's him. I get close, and I am in shock.

His face is so swollen and looks like he couldn't open his eyes even if he wanted to. His nose is flattened and his right ear is lacerated, hanging on by just a small piece of flesh, barely covered by some gauze. The rest of his face is covered with dried blood. I don't recognize him. My brother, the one I spent over twenty-three years of my life with, I couldn't tell who he was. Tears form in my eyes. He is sleeping, and I couldn't contain myself. I cry, I cry because I don't know what will happen to my little brother, the person I was tasked to protect ever since I was a young boy, the person who looks up to me for advice, the person who sees me as a father figure at times.

"Why, God? Why him? Has he not been through enough?" I beg for something, anything from God. And yet he leaves me unanswered again. I have to compose myself, to pick myself up and at least be able to show him strength, to be somebody he can depend on. He wakes up moments after.

"Hey, big bro. I'm not looking too bad, huh?"

"Honestly, you look better this way. What else are we waiting on?"

"I have to wait for the doctor to stitch up this ear"

"All right. Let me go find somebody and see if there's anything else we're missing."

I look for the doctor, a nurse, just somebody who seems to know what's going on and ask if they can see my brother. I finally get a hold of a receptionist,

"Hey, my brother is in room 303, and we are waiting for a doctor to see him. I just got here so I don't know what else we're supposed to do."

"Oh well let me check and see what the MA has put on the report…Looks like we are waiting for some MRI results."

"Oh, and what about his ear? Are they going to stitch him up?"

"I believe so. The doctor has a few more patients to see and then he'll be right over to check on him."

"Ok, I guess we just have to wait then. Thank you."

When I'm back, I see his girlfriend there.

"Hey, I'm Jessica. I hoped to have met you under different circumstances. Haha." She laughs nervously, as if not knowing how to react to what just happened. I feel the same way.

"Haha. It's ok. Thanks for taking care of my brother. I appreciate it."

As I say those words, my eyes water, but I hold the tears in.

In the midst of the chaos, I forget that my love was working graveyard shift that night. So I look for her for some consolation.

"Hey."

"Hey."

"My brother is in the hospital right now"

"What happened? Is he going to be ok?"

"I don't know. I'm still waiting for the doctor to come by and let me know what's going on."

"I'm sorry, babe. How does he look?"

I send her a picture of him and she replies, "Oh wow. How did this happen?"

Even I wasn't too sure, but from the small details I could at least paint a picture.

"He was out at a bar after his shift. He went outside to see what was going on, and then next thing he knows there's four guys beating on him."

"I'm sorry. How are you feeling?"

"Honestly, I'm a mix between furious and sad. I don't know what to feel right now. I just have to keep a strong front for my brother."

"Do you need anything?"

"I just need a hug."

"I'm sorry."

"Oh…ok"

I knew she was working, and I knew she had other responsibilities. But one hug was all I needed from her. I just wanted one hug to not exhaust my emotional health to keep up this front. I know it might've been too much to ask, but it left me feeling dull again. I worked so hard to work past that, but it came back in moments. All it needed was a moment of weakness from me. I told myself, "Fine, then I handle this the old way. Hopefully for the last time."

We wait close to an hour but a nurse finally comes to the room to finish stitching up his ear. I can barely stand to see it as the nurse tries and to handle the loose skin. She first needs to numb the area and the pain from the anesthetic makes my brother tears up. I have to look away. Each stitch seems to cause pain to Carlos, and I can't do anything but hold his hand through it. Every time the nurse punctures my brother with the needle he grips my hand tighter and tighter.

"Just a few more bro. Only a few more stitches."

"I don't know if I can take any more, bro."

"You have to. It's all right, I'm right here. You got this."

"All right. Let's get this over with."

The nurse finishes up the stitches and we both breathe a sigh of relief.

The nurse says, "All right that's all done. I know it wasn't fun but thanks for staying tough and sticking through it. The MRI results should be done soon and the doctor will let you know what's next."

We both respond, "Thank you."

"All right bro, we still got some time to chill so just take a nap and I'll let you know when we can head out."

His girlfriend comments, "Umm, he's already sleeping."

We both chuckle a little bit.

"Good, he deserves a bit of rest. You don't have to stay if you don't want to. I got it from here."

"You sure?"

"Yeah, he's my brother. I'll take care of him."

"Ok. Let me know when you guys are back at his place."

"Ok."

During these hours I feel the entirety of pain, of rage, of sadness. I know there is not an ounce more I can feel. I grow hyper aware and it makes this wait feel like an eternity. I compose myself again as the doctor comes in, and I pay attention to every word he says.

"All right the MRI looks ok, he doesn't have any severe damage brain damage so that's definitely a plus. He will need to see a plastic surgeon for his nose to get reconstructed. I can't do anything about that here. I'll refer you to somebody. He'll be prescribed some painkillers and anti-inflammatories for the swelling and any residual pain. Just follow the directions on the bottles. And that ear will need to be cleaned at least twice a day to make sure it doesn't get infected. You got all of that?"

"Yes, Doctor. Is there anything else I need to know?"

"Nope, that should be it. Once I send the prescription to the pharmacy you should be good to go."

"Thank you for all the help, Doctor."

"No problem. I'm sure he'll heal up soon."

"I hope so."

It is close to 7AM, and I am finally able to take my brother back to his place. He passes out instantly again. I took charge and go straight to get his meds and work on getting his appointments set up for his nose and eyes. The damage is severe. Three bone breaks around the eye sockets, a completely shattered nose, a concussion, and obviously the lacerated ear. I took the police report and took down the officer's information.

I call my parents, I have no emotion in my words, and I merely state the facts and let them feel what they need to. By the time they get there, all they need to do is sit and watch him sleep. I change my schedule to make sure that I can be there for the weekend to take care of him. My parents come by and see him. They are both composed as they see my brother.

My mom turns to me and says, "Thank you for taking care of your little brother. We love you." She proceeds to hug me and cry on my shoulders.

"It's ok, Mom. He'll be all right."

I say those words with full confidence. I am cold and calculated. I know how to present myself to my parents and to my brother. I know what needs to be done and what words need to be said to them. My objective is to make this as painless as possible for all of them. And that's why I volunteered to stay and watch over him for the weekend. I don't need my parents always worrying about his every step. He is still human, and he needs freedom, too. So I detach myself again, to not even see myself as his brother, solely a human whose mission is to help this other human.

Saturday, he is incoherent most of the day as he is tired. He didn't sleep all day Friday as he needs to take his initial meds in a timely manner. I care for his bandages, clean his ears, and make him meals. I do all that so I can to make sure he rests as much as possible.

He thanks me as he says, "Thanks, bro. I don't think I would have let Mom or Dad take care of me like this. I don't want them to freak out. Honestly, ever since I moved out, I see you more like a dad to me."

Those words break me from that façade for a moment as I appreciate his words. I know he means them, and it gives me a bit of a flashback to a few weeks prior to when my love told me something similar.

"No problem, bro. You know I'm here for you. Now let me clean that ear."

I quickly patch up that façade and go back to work. I make sure he was doing ok and message the rest of the family with updates. There is nothing else anybody needs to do. I take care of it. Sunday is much of the same thing, but he has had enough time for what happened to soak in. He recognizes what has happened to him.

By the end of the day, before I leave for the night, he asks, "Hey, can I get a hug?"

"Sure, come here."

As we embrace, he hugs me tight and then whispers in my ears as he sobs, "Why me, bro? Why me?"

My heart drops to the floor. I want to cry with him but know there was only room for him to do so. I have to hold in my tears once again and stay composed, hoping my façade doesn't shatter before I leave. I respond, "Hey, it's all right. It's all right."

I hug him not like a brother at that moment, but as a father. I have no other words to say. There is nothing to say. I just witnessed my brother's soul break in front of me. The only thing I can do is hold on to him, hoping that it will allow his heart to hold on to all those pieces of his shattered spirit. That's all I could do. The shock of his soul shattering makes ripples that affected mine. I do not understand his physical pain, but at that moment I hear the cries not just of his outer self but that of his inner self as well.

From that, I grow distant from everybody, especially my love. I don't know how to react, and I find it hard to break that cycle I purposefully dive back into. It feels like in a matter of weeks, I start to become the same being I was at the start of this journey. But I have always been positive towards my love. I feel as though it is divine, but I am in a realm that it will not reach me.

"Hey, are you doing ok?"

"Yeah, I'm fine. Why?"

"You seem different, ever since you had to take care of your brother."

"Oh, how do I seem different? I don't feel it."

"You just seem too serious. I think you should try and focus on what you told me, finding your dream. Maybe it will help take your mind off of things."

"My dream? I've been trying, but everything I've been doing hasn't helped. I'm still in the same spot as before."

"Well, maybe you need to try something different. You can't expect to be somewhere new if you haven't done anything new."

"What do you think I should do, though?"

"Read a book. Or maybe write a book. I love the letters you send me, and I always think their well thought out. Maybe try it."

"I don't know. It's easy to write you letters, but a full book. I don't know if I can."

"Stop being so negative."

"Sorry. I'll think about it."

"Do more than think. Try it. You're stuck in your head too much already."

"Yeah." I say in a somber tone.

"Whatever. Just do what you want. It's your life"

I feel like I have just been betrayed by life, by God. I turn to her to fill me with something, just a speck of hope to keep me from diving into the void. It is naïve of me to do so as it only slows her down on her own journey. I don't know how to feel, so I don't, just like before. It grows some resentment in her as she believed I was only criticizing her actions, even though all I really wanted to convey was my concern, to make sure she was safe.

The tension between us grows because of it, and then one fated day, she makes her peace and says, "I'm done. I don't want to do this with you anymore."

My heart shatters immediately. I am too naïve to realize that I am the one to drive her to that decision. I don't know what to say. "I'm sorry."

That's all I could muster up. I am holding back the tears as I see her in front of me. I can't believe that after the highs and the lows it would end so suddenly. What is only a few seconds feels like an eternity of torture. For my heart finally had something of substance, but it was short-lived. It tried to preserve something for too long and soiled the fruits of our labor. I finally find a bit or courage to muster up a few words,

"If you truly think this is done, then please, take the things that are yours from my house. I won't need them anymore."

She responds, "Hmm."

I don't know what that meant. It throws my mind into even more confusion. I stay as composed as I can while she is in front of me, and as she leaves, I break down. Tears do not run through my face, for I am still in shock, but I drop to my knees as the weight of my body pulls me to the ground.

"Is this the price I pay for love? Is this truly what I had to pay? God, please answer me. What else do you need to see?" Silence fills the room again.

.

Reconciliation

DISDAIN FILLS MY TASTE BUDS. How much longer will I feel this anger? I've let it consume me for one too many moments. The adrenaline I have coursing through my veins makes me feel more beast than man. This feeling, so reminiscent, I cast it out long before I met her, but it has come back to fuel me once again.

I need to express this, so I go to the one place that allows me to do so, the gym. An orchestra of violence plays in my head as I want not to merely move weights, but to feel murderous intent in my hands. I want to exhaust all my resources here and now in a final act of war. I want it to be recognized such as a gladiator in the colosseum fighting the vicious lion for what may be his last days. I form myself as the gladiator and the weights housed my adversary, which is the pitiful sight of me lying on the dirt, waiting for somebody to save me. But I know that salvation is for those who are in good standing with God, and He proved to me that I am not. Not a single word He could say to me. I move weights for what seemed to be hours. As I feel like I extinguished all of those flames, a new resurgence of it comes with the utterance of, "Not even worth a single word." My body comes to terms with the idea that this may be its last act. Hours of intensity pass and finally that fury, the adrenaline, it comes to an end. It might have been a small act of salvation but at the time it felt like God mocking me saying, "You do not deserve a glorious death. You must live here, with this regret for the rest of your days." It is disappointing.

The rage settles, and I become more coherent, and the thought that I lost her, and possibly the family I have yearned for, births a sadness so immense. I have felt this before, a sadness like this. It is formless, shapeless, covered in mystery. But now, it has a shape and a name. It has a definitive start and a climatic end. What do I do next? I find it difficult to ask, as I want to sulk in this sorrow for eternity. But I find it even more difficult to answer, as it cast a fire under my heart, and it still hurts from the burns of that rage. The day has turned to night, and I stay trapped in my bed. I feel paralyzed, "Move, just get up damnit. Get up, come on." Those words come from my persistent soul, it wants to go, to express itself, as it now feels like it has taken the backseat. Nothing happens, I stay in bed as I have no strength to do anything else. My mind, my body, my heart, they all lock my soul for the night.

I rapidly grow tired, as the hours are wasted away. My eyes close for what seems to be the first time in days, and I quickly go into a deep sleep. Maybe in my dreams I can find some solace, some peace. Maybe in my dreams I can finally have my words with God. The scene of my dreamscape quickly forms. It's night, in a familiar place, trees surround the skyline and have just enough luminosity from the moon. Thin clouds dance in the sky at times veiling the serene moon. The smell of the wind fills the atmosphere with comfort. My feet stand on top of a grass so soft

I would have guessed it to be pillows had I not looked down. The heat from the soil radiates up through my body and caresses my soul. This place feels like home, as it has the warmth of my mother's hug and the security of my father's presence. There is a slight fog that covers most of the horizon but as I focus more and more, it seems to scatter unveiling an ocean. From a close distance, I see a reflection of a light that plays with the water. "Is this…No, it can't be…" I proceed to turn around and look at the structure hovering over me. The lighthouse, the same one I saw many moons ago. The one thing that helped illuminate my path for so long. I stand at the base of the mountain that props it higher than any other feature in this entire place. It is too far from my eyes to make out any features besides its grandiose light.

However, just below it, there's a small overhang with a creature that rests on it, a lion. It resides as king over this domain as it proceeds to start the descent down the hillside to meet me, an intruder. I feel fear, not from any chance of physical harm, but fear from the possibility that he may cast me out of his domain. As he approaches, I can feel his presence more and more. His fur is made of gold and steals light from the moon to make it shine. His mane is full with a rich brown that resembles bronze. He makes his first steps at the base of the mountain and they shook the feet underneath me. His presence almost became too much for my body to handle as I wanted to collapse to my knees. My eyes keep focus on him, however. I can see his eyes are made of a ruby red that contrasted his black pupils. His gaze stays, locked onto me as he approaches with each step. Each step he took was serene, not making sound, but still had the impact that could shape this place if he so pleases. The colosseum of trees surrounds us and watches over as they expect a grand show unfold in front of their eyes. The closer he got to me, the more vibrant his fur coat, as it seemed like every hair had its own distinct color. The slight breeze allowed each strand of hair to flow in unison, making it seem like he was covered in a sea of gold. His tail terminated with a light flame that hovered just above the ground. I've never witnessed such a creature in my life, nor would I be capable of depicting one or dreaming of one like him. He was beyond my scope of creativity. This was a foreign being to me in all respects.

"**Who are you?**" His words stopped all the movement around him. They had such vigor that it almost caused my knees to buckle, but I somehow stayed firm.

"I don't know anymore."

"**This place has called you here. It only invokes the presence of those who it yearn to see. And yet you can't even tell it your name?**"

"I'm ___"

"**A nameless being. You have been here before, haven't you?**"

"Yes, but at the other side of the ocean, across the shoreline. It was at that place that I saw a glimpse of what was here."

"**And what do you believe to be here?**"

"Home."

"**Home is where one can find peace, and your presence here disturbs the peace that I have made in my domain. What makes you worthy of setting foot here?**"

"Nothing, I know of my nature, I am not worthy enough to set foot at this island anymore."

"**This place seems to think otherwise. For it too has a spirit and it sees the potential you house in your being. It has been calling for you ever since that fated day. I too have recognized** that. It has started to form a new mountainside, one where you were meant to reside in"

I look up at the ledge he presided over, and to the side of that a vacant one is there, just as he said. Has this place been yearning for me ever since that day?

"I will examine your being to see if you are truly worthy of that foothold just below the lighthouse."

He proceeds to rip off my shirt, and he stares at my chest focusing on the tattoo of a lion, a fake representation imparted on my skin through the pain of needles. Already I can feel his eyes judge me. But they do not sting as that of the dove. He places his paw on my chest and reads the calls of my heart and my soul.

"Hmmm, I see."

"What is it you see?"

"This place is right to notice your potential, for it is boundless. Your soul houses a fire that is unique in the way it burns and in the shape it takes. It burns in such elegant colors, as if burning gold, silver, sapphire, and many other precious items. You have inherited this from your mother, for she too holds a similar fire in her heart and she gave you a piece of it that you have molded to be your own. It craves this place, and even more, for it knows it can reach the heavens. But you have not yet examined yourself fully."

"What does that mean?"

"Your heart fights against your soul. It has a resolve and a strength that can weather all storms. It can hold the pieces of another's shattered heart and with the diligence so pure and detailed, it can help sew them all together again and protect it until it is ready to beat again. Your father gave you this he has shown you the willingness of the heart to thrive, to conquer, not matter how silent the man. But your heart craves comfort, something your soul can never accept. For it craves progress, and progress happens at moments of discomfort.

"You must reconcile these two pieces of yourself. For giving in to the fires of your soul will bring you an insatiable hunger, but allowing your heart to always take priority will lead you down a road of complacency.

"You have once believed that pain would be your only teacher in life, and although it has taught you much, it is not the only route to knowledge. Going through all that self-inflicted pain has made you disconnected with your heart and inherently this world.

"Love, you have experienced that recently, and it brought you the greatest of joys. But it has also brought to you the greatest of tragedies. Your heart was not ready for such passion, as it did not know how to control it. For you believed at the time that to love is to live, but I am here to tell you otherwise. You must live in order to love. You have imparted too much value in someone and it transcends your capabilities. So in spite, you begin to succumb to those old demons named insecurity and regret. But know this, young soul, demons cannot die of mortal hands.

"You stand before me a broken man once again. You have finally tasted all the soiled fruit of your misguided philosophy. You have asked me once before to show you the depths of your pain, and this is it. You have nothing in front of you. You have no partner, no real philosophy in life, your soul is shattered once again, and your body is tearing apart, and your heart is barely beating. But stay standing, persevere once more, for this time, if you stay true to these words, you will be able to take my spot in this domain."

"But what of you? What of that other ledge? Who is to fill that spot?"

"My place is much greater than these grounds, my place is one that hovers above all in this realm. One day I will see you at my home, and we will converse about the path you have decided to take from here. This is your new starting point.

"The other ledge is for you to decide. You can fill this spot with whoever you desire, but your heart speaks to me with no shroud of doubt. She is the one you want there, isn't she?"

"Yes. Of course, I do."

"Then if she is the one you truly desire here, never lose the flame in your soul. And never give in to hers as she will never give in to yours. Rebuild yourself again and find her. That tree you held so closely to still holds on to life. Take it, plant it here, and make sure it grows for it will be the path to my domain."

"Thank you. You have filled me with hope once again. What can I call you?"

"You know of my name. For I have been with you since the beginning. I have seen you grow into the being you are today. I have seen you before you were even born. This form is not my true form, only your depiction of me, one that allows you to engage with me."

Instantly, I knew who He was. I felt ashamed that it took me this much to open my eyes to Him. That was what made me fall to my knees. The fact that I lost touch with Him, that fact that I resigned myself to hate Him for a moment in time and yet He still is here in front of me not willing to give up on me.

"How come you didn't recognize me when you laid eyes on me here?"

"A nameless being has no form. I needed to see inside your heart for myself to make sure you are who I believed you to be."

"How come you were never there, how come you never answered me?"

"Were you ready to listen even if I did answer? The cracks in your ego were enough to sliver in a few words at the beach. They have filled you with enough vitality to make it this far, but life forced you to close your shell to me again. So ever since then I have been waiting patiently for this day. I have been there hovering over your shoulders waiting for the last bit of pride, the last layer of ego to peel off so that you could hear these words for once."

"I'm sorry it took so long. I'm sorry I wasn't ready back then. I'm sorry. I'm sorry."

It feels like all that pain is slowly being exorcised from my being through these tears I shed. I am grateful. He has finally showed me of the depths of this pain for once. The tears dry out, and I regain my composure as some of His wisdom begins to be imparted on me.

"You now know why I cannot intervene, for this is your test of faith, not mine. For me to be able to judge you at your last days fairly, I cannot interfere. Now go, young soul. Begin anew and rebuild yourself to something greater, something that even the oceans cannot contain. Rebuild and unlock your full potential. I will be here at the shoreline waiting for you once more."

I wake up as He finishes those last words. My body again is battered, but my destiny is calling me. I need to get up and rebuild my soul once more, this time with the aid of my own heart. Although I am broken again, He has awoken my dream and it has breathed life into me. To think I have to start from the exact same spot, but this time, I'm ok with it. I'm ok with starting from scratch. I will overcome those demons, but with His help. And my love, I will take her with me. Our story is not yet finished. It is only about to begin. So I call her the second I get out of bed. I don't get an answer, so I leave a voicemail

"Hey. I don't expect you to respond to this, but I need to tell you something. I'm coming back. I'm going to make myself better, and I want to show you who I'm going to become. I won't change for you. I'm not, I can't. I'm going to change for myself, but you will be there as my greatest motivation in case I want to dive back into the person I was. I know that I might have lost you forever. I know that I might never get the chance to hold you in my arms or kiss you. I know that possibility. But I'm going to try and give this everything I have to show you what my soul is made out of. I know now what I did wrong. I didn't support you as I should have. I didn't help you get through the hurdles you needed to get through. But this time around, I'll be here for anything and everything. Whatever it is, I'm going to help in any way I can. So, don't slow down on your own dreams, I will catch up. I have rested for too long, but soon I will be at your side again."

I hear nothing for a few hours. I didn't even think that she would respond. So I continue on with the day with the pain in my chest, the pain that I won't run away from. It's a pain that I need to embrace, and I will do so gladly. It's soothing, for the pain I feel I know is what is mending my heart and my soul. They are finally at peace with each other. They may both be worn and broken, but at least, for once, they can live simultaneously. And the irony is that I feel alive. I understand now what it means to feel alive. I move forward now because I want to live, not because I have been willing to die. I clear my house of the things I bought my love, and as I do, I see my old journal. I never wrote much in it, but I still kept it. The last entry was two years ago and it was nothing of importance. But I put it down next to my bed as I want to write in it again, as she wanted me to. I am ready to relieve myself from her, to let go of all the memories and all the love as I take all these things and am just about ready to throw it all away. Then, I feel my phone buzz. She responds to my voicemail message and texts,

"I don't know if I can believe you. But I want to. I really do. But we'll see if it's true."

"Yeah. You will."

"<3"

I bring back the trash bag of all of her gifts that I bought her. I store them in my closet for now. She will be mine again, I am sure of it. So now I pick up the pen and begin to write.

– END

Made in the USA
Coppell, TX
18 May 2022

77914347R00142